THOUGHT *the Greatest Power of All*

Thought
the
Greatest
Power
of All

Héctor Amézquita

 DEVORSS Publications

© 1997 Héctor Amézquita

ISBN: 0-87516-708-X

Library of Congress Catalog Card Number 97-67730

DeVorss & Company, *Publishers*
Box 550
Marina del Rey, CA 90294

Printed in the United States of America

To all the spiritual beings who are
now having human experiences!

Contents

My Essence Is My Fire Within

Yes, I have a fire within
like the magma inside the living planet Earth.

      It's the burning Sun in my inner universe
      that keeps me warm when it's cold outside.

It's the fire within that touches everyone else,
the same fire within all living things
that touches me when I get close to them.

      It's the same fire that created the Universe,
      the Big Bang that made of it the body of God,
      the house we all inhabit.

It's the same fire that melts the minerals,
that makes me feel love for the newborn's expression
and Love for the fire Itself.

      Of course, I didn't ask for this—
      because I was
      and I have always been
      my essence, my Fire within!

HÉCTOR AMÉZQUITA

Preface

21 YEARS ago my conscious mind began to realize that there were, at a very deep level of awareness within my being, the memories of an essential ignorance, some kind of alertness about a missing piece of knowledge —knowledge about which I needed to become consciously aware.

A lot of concern and restlessness was raised after this recognition. I needed more than ever to find the missing piece, *because I always knew there was something else* but did not know where and how to start finding it. Probably reading more, studying more, asking more, I thought. And I did.

Years of research, of patient effort, and it happened! I found the right books and met the right people. Both sources provided the information I was looking for.

The outcome: *I found the missing piece. It was in me!* Nowhere else. The missing piece was within me. And *as* me, *was* me; the real me. It was my inner self. My Higher Self!

O God! I found you! Let me express my overwhelming thankfulness for my knowing of this truth, this magnificent truth. Now I am consciously aware that God is Spirit,

Truth, Love, Life, Thought, Good, Peace, Light, Mind, Energy, Power. All there is! And ALL this manifests through me and all of us!

Isn't this great?

Now I also know with certainty, I confirm and ratify, that this is what I always wanted to share: this knowledge, this conscious awareness of who we really are! I need to share all this with you, word for word, together with a description of what has helped me to change my life for the better, to find myself where I am. I will share with you everything, with the sincere desire that it will do for you all the good that it has done for me.

Acknowledgments

There are no words with adequate meaning to express my profound gratefulness to all those who, in one way or another, helped me to write, complete and publish this book. I am much indebted to all of them.

I hereby acknowledge those special individuals whose names I remember and all those whom I might unwittingly be overlooking:

Jennifer Shenkman, who gave me the first support in the editing field; and, with special gratitude, Rafe Stephan, whose contribution in editing was influential before I went to my publisher.

In a not lesser position my son, Tony Amézquita, whose editing efforts and comments about the contents of the book provided valuable feedback; my dear friend and neighbor, Bob Wood, whose patience and experienced understanding of life gave me three years of support with his honest and unconditional friendship; my many years' good friend Alex Williams, in addition Director of the first Study Group of Religious Science in Guatemala, whose also pertinent comments on the contents of the book added additional necessary input; and finally, my good friends: Nadja Frau, Sonia Nieves, Dion Koch, and Joan Dick, whose varied contributions and comments largely contributed to support the book's contents.

I know there are no accidents. I can see how all the events and persons were in the right place at the right time to provide their contributions. Such is the case with Gary Peattie, Arthur Vergara and Hedda Lark of DeVorss & Company, who were part of the right opportunity to publish and distribute *my first book!*

Thank you all.

Introduction

W HY do so many human beings, although they are not actually sick, find themselves trudging through life joylessly and unsmilingly, unable thoroughly to enjoy the simple fact of being where they are, when they are? Many go through their lives in sorrow, unaware of the truth about themselves just because they learned wrong ideas and adopted wrong beliefs. They probably are unaware of certain basics such as WHO, WHAT, WHERE, WHEN and WHY they are.

These unfortunate ones do not know that their identity, the "WHO they are," is a manifestation of a Universal Intelligence, an amazing concentration of the purest intelligence and energy imaginable. These were contained within an immensely concentrated, diminutive body known as "singularity," as scientists term it, that exploded some 15 billion years ago, creating the whole Universe, including time and space, which we humans are beginning to explore and understand.

A part of this Universal Intelligence is temporarily inhabiting human physical bodies in an environment named planet Earth. It is within those bodies—yours, mine, everyone's.

Most of us do not understand WHAT we are: *"Spiritual beings having human experiences."* We are unaware that we are within a body that is within a planet that belongs to a planetary system within one of the galaxies of that Universe created by the same Intelligence. This Universe is not something foreign to us "spiritual beings having human experiences." We are integral parts of it. WHERE we are, WHENever we are, on this planet or in another place in this Universe, can always be identified as "Here." And we are in that "Here" only "Now," simply because in the Universe, time as we know it does not exist.

And finally, many of us do not seem to know WHY we are here. We have not been able to identify our purpose as human beings; we have no direction for our lives. Perhaps we do not even know what we want to do while experiencing this human existence and, lacking information and proper understanding, have already lost control over our lives!

In this book you will find some of the answers to these five important aspects—the *who*, *what*, *where*, *when* and *why*—of human life.

During my many travels and experiences, I have observed so many individuals plodding without joy through lives devoid of true satisfaction or well-being. They simply are unaware of the moment in which they are living. Their minds remain in the past, re-experiencing events that may never happen again. Or their minds dwell in a future that has not yet happened and may never happen. They fail to realize that they are wasting the present moment, losing the opportunity of being aware of what they are experiencing. I say *wasting* and *losing* because from our physical point of view, this present moment will be gone forever, unnecessarily wasted, unnecessarily lost.

Why is it that so many people cannot easily enjoy what is going on in this moment, commonly called the here and now? Could it be that they do not know that the moment they waste so willingly is all the life they have, the only possession they have, and also the only opportunity they have to enjoy life as humans?

This book, dear reader, is dedicated to exploring and manifesting the potential for richness and beauty in each of those glorious moments of ours. It is a guide for those wishing to open their eyes to their own vast potential. It is a contribution to the never-ending process of self-improvement that is so essential for keeping the pace of natural evolution. I have invented nothing and I present nothing new. But I wish to share with you the ideas and concepts that have burst upon my life to change it so dramatically. A root cause of major human problems is the fact that so many of us learned *what* to think instead of *how* to think.

Knowing *how* to think involves conscious awareness of truth, learning new ways of thinking, and making the decision to be very careful of *what* we think. Knowing *how* to think liberates us to use our total freedom of conscious choice. Instead of being dominated by unwanted thoughts that arise in the absence of something better, the mind can easily be trained to think only what we allow it to think. We already know how to do this, but every time we want to stop thinking about something we do not like, we cannot easily change that thought—or can we?

The trouble is that we are not used to exercising our unlimited freedom of choice to determine our thoughts. We learned to think automatically, spontaneously. We need to start selecting our thoughts and managing them. Everything we do is preceded by a thought. Our thoughts are the producers of our present and the builders of our future. If we want to be the producers, directors and stars of the film called *Living on Planet Earth*, we must learn *how* to think.

As we think, we create our world in the here and now. In the life process, the inputs are our thoughts; the process itself is what we do (our interpretations, actions and reactions); and the outputs are our happiness or unhappiness. Computer jargon uses the expression "Garbage in—garbage out." And so it is with ourselves and our minds. If we put poor-quality thoughts into our minds, we get poor-quality lives. On the other hand, if we think upon what is *Universal Good*, we put in our lives love, health, abundance, wisdom and joy.

Because I am convinced that everything in my life is the outcome of my thoughts at conscious or subconscious levels, I have decided to learn how to think. It is my hope that this book will help you to gain access to your own ways of *how* to think. Remember, you are free to think anything, but not everything is good for you to think. You may poison your mind, your body and your life if you are not truly careful in using your freedom to choose your thoughts. When you understand the difference between *what* and *how* to think, you become willing to create change as a most natural outcome; and *change is natural and leads to growth*.

We are what we think we are. A person who says, "I am not happy because I was born in a dysfunctional family," appears to be telling the truth. However, she is unhappy because of *what* she thinks, not because she was born in a dysfunctional family. She cannot be happy as long as she continues this direction of thinking. Many individuals have been born in dysfunctional families and are happy now. I am one. On the other hand, many individuals who were born in supposedly functional families are unhappy. The question here is: How many functional families actually exist? What *is* a functional family? Very few individuals actually believe their families are entirely functional.

Many use their dysfunctional families, or some other excuse, to justify their lack of ability, or their unwillingness, to learn *how* to think. They do not understand that they exercise total freedom in choosing the way they feel and the way they live. They do not understand that current and past events do not determine the way they have to feel now, unless they freely decide to do so. It is the same with events they mentally locate in the future, because those events do not determine the way they have to feel now unless, again, they freely decide to do so. This means that they can feel either miserable or delighted anywhere and any time they decide to do so.

There is a lot to learn. But first we must come to a deep understanding of *how* to think. We must then be willing to use this understanding to liberate ourselves and to make deep, fundamental changes in our lives. The changes we make will allow us to identify effectively our individual purpose in this world and, better yet, to accomplish it. Those changes will fulfill our innermost desires because they all mean growth. We need to reverse the effect of unconsciously being against ourselves!

Mark Twain said, "It's not what you don't know that hurts you. It's what you do know that ain't so." I agree that lack of knowledge might not hurt us, but I suggest that we create a mechanism that we can call the "unlearning process." Let us unlearn all that unnecessarily hurts us. And let us replace it with new knowledge that will benefit us with its presence.

Dear reader, please understand that I am writing about the way I see things. I do not pretend to have the best formula or the only formula. What I present to you is the formula that works for me—one that enables me to live in a permanent state of peace, happiness, enthusiasm and joy for life.

It could be that some of us are afraid of change, but we

have to start realizing that everything in the physical environment is constantly changing and that change is absolutely vital. Changing old ways of thinking may enable you to enjoy the rest of your life far more than you ever had expected. Almost anyone, when asked, would declare that they would love to become a famous artist. You may become an artist by just awakening and releasing that artist within you! Make living an art, and then make a piece of art out of the rest of your life!

1

Purpose

I BELIEVE our purpose as human beings is to raise our consciousness to understand the total freedom with which we are empowered and use it to experience our inner self, our Higher Self—to experience the Creative Universal Intelligence and then express It. Most of us at one point fail to understand that this Universal Intelligence does not play favorites among us; that we all are created equal, that we are provided with exactly what we need to have happy human experiences; and that all outcomes are the result of the use we make of our unlimited freedom.

Using our unlimited freedom during our evolutionary process, we humans have created a large number of wrong beliefs that have become paradigms (patterns or models) for us. These wrong beliefs have been transmitted from one generation to the next because it is only now that many of us are beginning to be more concerned with *how to think* and how to use our unlimited freedom, rather than with the *what to think* that is the legacy of previous generations. Still, many of us tend to sustain most of the following beliefs:

1. There is God, with an anthropomorphic appearance, everywhere outside us.
2. We have to fear God in order to be good humans.

3. If we do something wrong, God will punish us.
4. An evil entity exists that promotes human wrong-doing.
5. We need to belong to a religious group to have spiritual experiences.
6. We must go to churches to find God.
7. When we die, we go to heaven or hell, depending on how we lived.
8. Our life is only our physical-body experience, with a probable soul (which nobody has proved to exist).
9. Only those who profess our beliefs will be saved.
10. What others do or do not do is the cause of our happiness or unhappiness.
11. Our needs are to be filled by others.
12. Taking care of ourselves first, as individuals, is selfishness.
13. Planet Earth is the center of all the Universe. We can watch the Universe in the back yards of our houses.
14. We live in the day of the month of the year indicated in the calendar.
15. Resenting negative events that occurred in the past might allow us a chance to change them.
16. Preoccupation with the future might help us decide it.

Reading, studying and learning *how* to think has changed my entire life. Based on my experiences, I can make the following specific declaration:

I now have come to believe:

1. The power, or the source of the power, that created the entire universe, including our small planet and its different expressions of life, is what we humans call God, the Universal Mind, the Universal Spirit. What else could

possibly have created all the wonders you can see and all those you cannot see? This Universal Mind is ALL and is in us, within us—and, *as* us, *is* us! This means that each one of us is an individual expression of that Universal Power in our two streams of manifestation: the temporary physical and the eternal immortal spiritual.

2. Humans as individual manifestations of God on earth are created differently from one another, but all with the same resources and the same total freedom to think and do. At a deeper level, we all are one with each other and with the Universal Spirit. And because Spirit or God is perfect and is love, It does not contain evil and does not create evil. There is no reason for us to fear God in order to be good human beings. We are *essentially* good. There are not two powers in the Universe, one good and one bad. There is only one absolute power that is all Good.

3. Misusing our total freedom, because of ignorance, we choose to do wrong things that affect ourselves and others; but we have to face the consequences of violating Universal Principles or human precepts. In other words, it is our own mistakes, our own wrongdoings that punish us, in one way or another; it is never the God of love that punishes us, the same God of love that created us. Wrongdoing is always punished by the Universal Law of Cause and Effect.

4. There is no evil entity leading humans to err, but the misuse of our total freedom, granted to us by God and little understood by us, does lead us astray. We need to *liberate* ourselves from wrong beliefs and learn *how* to think to avoid continuing misusing our individual freedom. This freedom bestows all kinds of liberties if we properly understand it; it is not a license or privilege for wrongdoing.

5. We can grow to experience God as we learn *how* to think and as we become experts at thinking in wiser ways that lead us to the Truth.

6. We can experience God in the here and now (anywhere we might be at any time) because God is around and within each of us. We do not go to churches to find God, but to increase our conscious awareness of God. There is but one altar, to which no church has exclusive rights, and that altar is in you, in each of us. It is an altar of the Highest Intelligence, which you already are!

7. When we die, we do not actually die; we only have a transition whereby we return the physical body we have been using as a vehicle for having our human experience. We then, I believe, move to other worlds, to other dimensions, to have higher experiences in a continuous evolutionary process.

8. Our life is eternal; what is temporary is our body. We may experience eternity at all times in all places as we learn to become consciously aware of it.

9. All humans are entirely free to search for the meaning of life. Nobody has a patented formula for "salvation." Salvation from what? There is nothing we need to be saved from, such as "hell," "purgatory," "damnation" and the like. Who or what could have created such things? A God of Love that is all Good?

10. We are not dealing with time, people, places, things, conditions or situations. We are dealing with ourselves, with our interpretation process. It is mostly based on the *what to think* we have learned, on the wrong be-

liefs we have adopted, our conditioning that we rarely question, and, because of this, we make wrong interpretations or interpretations that do not serve our lives well. The external reality is that others are not responsible for our happiness or unhappiness. We can be happy or sad depending on how we use our total freedom of choice to interpret what has happened, what is happening, or what might happen outside of ourselves. How we feel is determined by that use of our freedom.

11. My needs are to be fulfilled by myself alone, by my learning how to use the existing divine sources of supply. I must take responsibility for my life by learning how to think, how to heighten my ability to respond to myself and to others.

12. I owe it to my loved ones to take good care of myself first, to give myself the best first and to demonstrate the peace and the happiness I am intended to possess for my complete understanding of the Universe. For how can I share with my loved ones and others something I do not have?

13. The "singularity,"* as defined by the scientific community, that created the Universe is God. The entire Universe and all its contents is the Oneness and the Allness of God. We exist within the Universe, within God.

14. We live only in the here and now, because there is no time as we know it. What we know as measurements

*"Before the singularity there was nothingness. At a mathematical point of 0-space with infinite density of ? appears a singularity, which is pure energy. No explanation of how it was created." (From E. Karel Velan, *The Origin of the Universe*.)

of time are created by us to enable us to understand the framework within which events occur.

15. By resenting events in the past, we generate emotions such as guilt, shame or anger. The only two good things that can be done are: to forgive others and ourselves, and to change the interpretation of the past event, identifying and remembering the lesson that is always there.

16. It is useless to be preoccupied with the future. We are best served by simply developing a clear vision of what we want in our future. This will give direction to our lives and meaning to our daily living—some good thing to be occupied with instead of being only ''preoccupied.'' Our preoccupation will vanish as our faith and knowledge develop.

You may agree with me that the first list can be substituted for the second, either totally or in part, as you see fit. The fact is that this material has already given us a lot of topics for discussion.

If you are resisting these ideas or you feel yourself a little skeptical, let me suggest that you might be going through a *paradigm effect*, responding to a model from your previous or still prevailing beliefs. You can overcome this effect because, like an external event, a paradigm or belief will only affect you to the extent that you allow it to.

If the above has provoked you to question how I dare to write some of these things, I invite you to continue with me as I demonstrate that with good will and some effort we may come to know the truth that will liberate us, just as Jesus told us we could. We will then be able to use our total freedom in a limitless way.

2

How to Think vs. What to Think

I GNORING truth is as harmful as believing untruths. We have a great need for accurate knowledge that will produce genuine wisdom. Generations of people have inherited limited information to build an accurate and reliable system of beliefs. This should not keep us from identifying techniques to build better belief systems. A large number of major beliefs simply are not accurate. Why is it so hard for so many of us to see this? Let us take a careful look at three specific examples:

1. Remember how earlier civilizations believed that Earth was a kind of a flat platform that ended beyond the seas? Remember how people used to fear that anybody who ventured to navigate to the borders of that platform would risk falling into the void? This was the way European civilization was thinking at the end of the fifteenth century. The paradigm shift took place when the American continent was discovered and it was confirmed that Earth was in fact a planet, a globe.

2. People used to believe that the sun and the stars circled the platform known as Earth, which remained still without any movement. There was no way to convince

them that in addition to not being a platform, Earth was a planet orbiting the sun.

Galileo Galilei was seriously threatened because he made public his observations confirming that Earth was, with other planets, orbiting the sun. All people needed to do at that time was to come out of their houses and confirm with their own eyes that the assertion that Earth was orbiting the sun was false, because they could easily see how the sun was instead orbiting Earth. It has taken many years to convince people of the truth. Can you imagine for a moment what the reaction would have been if the people of that time had been told that Earth travels with the sun in space at the speed of 700,000 miles per hour? Even now many people tend to disbelieve this truth.

3. Wayne W. Dyer, quoting the mathematician Douglas Hofstadter, tells us in his book *Real Magic* the following extremely illustrating short story:

A father and his son are driving to a football game. They come to a railroad crossing, and when it is halfway across, the car stalls. Hearing a train coming, the father desperately tries to get the engine started again. He is unsuccessful and the train hits the car. The father is killed instantly, but the son survives and is rushed to a hospital for brain surgery. The surgeon on entering the operating theater, turns white and says, "I cannot operate on this boy. He is my son."

What happened here? Can you make a guess before we continue? Could you tell what is the relationship between the dead father, the surgeon and the boy? This is a good illustration of a paradigm effect. If you do not know the answer already, let me provide it: *The surgeon is the boy's mother.*

If you are one of the rare people who realized right

away that the surgeon was the boy's mother, or you knew this story, you're probably pretty close to being in the right, or receptive, frame of mind. If you did not, but are willing to believe that there are many other seemingly impossible or implausible things that are in fact true—if you are willing to open your mind to entirely new ways of looking at your life and the events that surround it—you too are very close to being in the right frame of mind. So open your mind as wide as you possibly can, and follow me.

Now let us revise three of the ways in which we ourselves have missed some invaluable truths:

1. Recall our noting on p. 1 that many people believe God exists somewhere outside them. This is what they learned! Because this is all they had available at the time they were learning. They direct their prayers to an external God, who is somewhere "up there." They look to the sky, to the roof, to the church altar, or to an imaginary high place where God is supposed to be instead of looking for God within, at the center of their being. Each of us is a kind of a branch of God, like a little branch on a big tree—even though we are all, together with the entire universe, contained within God! We are extensions of God!

We all know God is everything, and we are included in that everything; so God is also in us—and, *as* us, *is* us! All the Universe is God. All that we are is God, but God is more than what we are. God is the creating source from which we emerge as the creation. We are created by God in Its image and likeness, yet God is not created by us. God is! It is not hard to accept the fact that God is within us. We know this truth intuitively. But because we only learned *what* to think and are afraid to challenge the learned "truth" and cannot find support for our natural inner feeling of the reality that God is within us, we choose to do nothing.

2. Also, on page 2, we noted: "What others do or do not do is the root cause of our happiness or unhappiness." Many believe their source of happiness or unhappiness is in what others think about them or in how others treat them, or in what others do or do not do, or in what happens externally. They have never learned how to respond to outside events through a correct interpretation of them, but instead they learned to depend on others or on external events or conditions for their sense of well-being and fulfillment.

It is very easy to confirm this extreme belief when you hear expressions such as, "The weather is getting me down" or "He makes me angry" or "She makes me happy" or "What will people think of me?" They fail to realize they are individuals who can freely, at any time, decide how to react, feel and respond, independently of any external event or condition, after correctly interpreting what *is* happening outside of themselves. The way they decide to react induces the way they feel and consequently the way they might respond, even if they do not manifest that response externally. The external event or condition does not cause the way one reacts, feels and responds. *We ourselves* decide the reaction, the feeling and the response, whatever it may be, after the interpretation we make of the external event or condition.

We imitate parents, relatives and peers who become upset or disappointed when others fail to conform to their expectations. They learned to blame "someone else" for their own reactive emotions, based on their own interpretations, which could be entirely false. The proof is easy.

An external event will arouse different reactions in different individuals, precisely because interpretations of what is perceived differ from one person to another. An event said by one to cause unhappiness should cause unhappiness to all and not only to some, whereas another event said to cause happiness to some is also said to have caused unhappiness to others.

3. Again on page 2, we indicated that many individuals believe that taking care of themselves first is selfish and undesirable. The suggestion that they might give themselves the best and make themselves feel well first, before taking care of others, induces for many an immediate sense of guilt. For example, many parents, particularly mothers, consider the most important persons in their family to be their children. They even say they are willing to sacrifice themselves for their children, which sounds meritorious, except for the fact that these same sacrificial candidates often scream at their children and spank them because of their own failure to feel good about themselves before interacting with their outside world (their children).

They are not taking care of their own selves *first*. They are not responding to themselves *first*. And of course *they cannot give what they don't have.* They do not realize they owe it to their loved ones to maintain themselves at their best. A mother who cares for herself before she takes care of others will not scream and spank, but will act with serenity, patience, understanding and loving care. The same applies to a husband, father, wife, friend, partner, peer, colleague.

The *what to think* we learned must be replaced with a commitment to learn *how to think*, so that we may respond to ourselves first, before we respond to others. Married people who have developed the ability to respond individually to themselves first, in the highest possible way, do not need their partners to share the accumulated frustrations of the day—because they will not have any! They are in a positon of always sharing well-being and happiness simply because they are responsible to themselves first. They got the well-being and the happiness first.

The father, mother, son, daugther, friend, colleague, partner, boss and subordinate all need to respond to themselves first, to get themselves in good shape first, before they respond to others. They must be able to deliver a response, by being response-able to themselves first. Their ability to respond has to be effective. This is not selfishness, this is responsibility.

If someone insists it is selfishness, then it is possibly the *positive side* of selfishness. If you do not clarify your thoughts first, how can you become a guide for others? How can you share a lesson you have not yet learned? How can you give something (love, peace, understanding) that you do not already possess? You must serve yourself first, become peaceful first, be complete first (do not be a half looking for another half), be response-able in a whole way! *Taking care of ourselves first is not selfish. It is a solemn responsibility.*

Those of us who have learned only *what to think* have only one way of understanding things and have a very limiting perspective on many important issues of life. You will later read in this book other very important examples of false beliefs or paradigms. I call them important because of the significance they have for the lives of individuals, not only for their private, but also for their professional and public, personae. For these reasons, we need to change the way we think. We all need to learn *how* to think, to open our minds to new ideas.

Take, for instance, the message of Pope John Paul II to the Pontifical Academy of Science, a lay organization meeting in Rome during the last quarter of 1996. The Pope said that new information has confirmed that Charles Darwin's theory of evolution is "more than a hypothesis." By not challenging the evidence that supports evolution, the Vatican positions the Roman Catholic viewpoint in contrast to that of some fundamentalist Christians who take the biblical account of Creation literally. At the same time it makes a sound paradigm shift by reflecting, in conclusion, the church's acceptance of Darwin's theory.

In the same fashion, we need to start challenging most of the things we learned, searching for new information that will lead us to establish in ourselves a *how to think* mechanism. Then we must develop an unlearning process for all those learned ideas that we can demonstrate are not true. I am positive we can add value to our lives if we seek knowledge that produces wisdom, through learning *how* to think. We can also add value to our lives by discarding beliefs we prove to be wrong.

We should start by identifying how we adopt our beliefs. From birth we observe what others do: how they behave, how they react. Because there is no optional information available, we conclude that what we are observing is the way to behave or to react. We probably determine that way is the only option and adopt it as a solid core belief. We perceive other persons' actions as the natural way to behave or to react and we unconsciously decide, when we like the action or the reaction and there is no option, that it is the right one. We adopt it as a belief or a *what to think* with some sense of loyalty. Subsequently we confirm that we made the right decision because we see other people doing the same thing; and, because nobody told us that there were other options, we never got to know those options.

Parents, teachers, churches, associations, authorities tell us *what to think*, what to believe, but nobody tells us *how to think*. Nobody explains the mechanism of proficient thinking, as that there is a difference between the concepts of *what to think* and *how to think*; and, of course, even if we sometimes get intuitive feelings that there is more, there is no easy way to confirm those feelings.

For instance, I did not like many things my father did or said, so I didn't adopt them as beliefs. However, I felt pleased with many other things he did or said and I adopted them as my beliefs. In several cases, I complemented some of them by adding conclusions of my own, and I ended up adopting the results as my beliefs. The same comment applies to my mother, my siblings, my relatives, my friends, the community and the like. I adopted beliefs from what they did or said, only when I liked what they did or said. I adopted beliefs from the information available regardless of how it reached me.

In a very involuntary way the others were telling me what to think and what to believe, not only because they did not know better, but also because unconsciously they wanted to be sure I was going to be the same as they were; they wanted to train me to behave and react the same way they did, to perpetuate their beliefs and traditions. They were preventing me from getting into the risky unknown. They were "teaching" me. I remember adults telling me how wise it was to get to know one's limitations to avoid getting in trouble. The outcome was that I created limitations. I used my creativity to develop limitations that I did not have, only because I accepted one of their wrong beliefs.

It seems that nobody tells us that we are free to think any way we want, to challenge anything and to feel any way we want. Curious as it may seem now, this happened to me when I was a child: my church did not want me to think on my own. The priest and fellow-congregants did not want me to question anything, but instead simply wanted me to accept what I was told. Around the early 1950s the Pope decided that Mary, the mother of Jesus, had, like Jesus, gone to heaven in body and soul. This declaration of Mary's bodily assumption into heaven, having the weight of dogma, had to be accepted without discussion. Blind obedience was considered a virtue. I decided to ask why ecclesiastical authorities waited 19 centuries to make that declaration on such an old and important event. The answer was that dogma should not be questioned. I was to believe as I was told to believe. I felt the whole idea was not very consistent with my judgment, but I decided to be obedient and believe as I was told.

The truth is that I never got to really believe that dogma. Nobody imposes beliefs on anyone. We adopt our beliefs in an extremely free fashion. It is useless to try to impose beliefs on anyone. Take a look at the following example: During my exchange of wedding vows in 1961 the priest included an admonition to my bride to "obey" her husband! Years after, in the course of a discussion typical of a married couple that had not yet learned how to think, I reminded my wife what the priest had said about her obligation to obey. How do you suppose she reacted?

My parents also wanted me to be obedient in order that I might be recognized as a well-mannered, civilized and obedient boy. From childhood I was trained to pay attention to the opinion of others—in other words, to external opinion. If we were going to visit another family, I was told to sit quietly, not to talk, not to interrupt, especially when adults were speaking, so I could be recognized as the good and obedient boy I was assumed to be. If I followed instructions, I was praised for my behavior. In this way I started learning to look for external approval.

When I was a child I heard expressions such as "I hate him" or "I hate her" and I asked: "How do you hate?" and I heard: "I don't know, but I hate him!" So, with practice, I learned how to hate when there was nothing to hate. Similarly, I learned to experience anger when there was nothing to be angry about; I learned how to contract diseases when there was no reason to lose one's health; I learned how to age when there was no need to get old, as Deepak Chopra proclaims in his books. Chopra asserts that: "The physical world (which includes our bodies), is a response of the observer. We create our bodies as we create the experience of our world." So we age because we *learned* to age. I learned to be afraid of "death," without knowing that we do not die—that we are immortal because eternal spiritual beings do not die; they are only having a human experience.

I adopted the beliefs available to me at the time I was learning—but, worse, I also learned to hold on to these and other similar wrong beliefs with tenacity. I was very often reminded to be consistent with my beliefs. I became unable to see the most helpful beliefs, even if they were clearly explained to me. The persons around me were defining my *what to think* in the future. I now interpret the involuntary messages as: "We don't want you to think by yourself, but to obey. What counts is the external approval, what people say. This is what you must think. If you think differently, you will be rejected." Besides, there was no one to tell me that the beliefs I was adopting were not the right ones.

Not many people tell you about the relationship be-

tween cause and effect. That would give you a much
clearer message on *how* to think. If you plant wheat, you
will get wheat. In the same way, if you plant wrong beliefs in yourself, you will have wrong thinking and wrong
choices later. If your thinking is based on what you have
learned and adopted as beliefs, based on what others have
previously thought, the outcome can very well be wrong
living, experiencing what you do not want to experience.

This is how we get our beliefs, so freely adopted, so
freely internalized! Then why is it that we so strongly resist
new ideas, refuse to change a belief, especially after we
are given compelling explanations that are eminently more
reasonable, more logical, and that make all kinds of sense
to our inner knowledge? This happens not only because
we came to believe what we were told to believe but also
because we had drummed into us that we must "stick to
our beliefs." We also learned to fear change, to fear the
unknown as we were becoming more and more affected
by the "paradigm effect."

Let us now talk about paradigms and their effects. The
word *paradigm* has been abundantly used in recent years,
but the number of individuals familiar with its use, meaning and effects is still limited. For this reason I want to explain that its current use began with Thomas Kuhn's book
The Structure of Scientific Revolutions, in which he in-
troduces us to the idea of the scientific paradigm. The
word comes from the Greek *paradeigma*, meaning "pat-
tern." Joel Arthur Barker in his book *Paradigms* con-
cludes that paradigms have a negative effect on those who
are unaware of them and on those who do not resist or
fight their effect. Paradigms can virtually make us blind
to an understanding of different, far more logical and
productive ways of thinking or acting, producing a tremendous waste of new or different ideas!

Barker provides many good examples of words that represent subsets of the paradigm concept: Theory, Model, Methodology, Principles, Standards, Protocol, Routines, Assumptions, Conventions, Patterns, Habits, Common Sense, Conventional Wisdom, Mindset, Values, Frames of Reference, Traditions, Customs, Prejudices, Ideology, Inhibitions, Superstitions, Rituals, Compulsions, Addictions, Doctrine and Dogma.

A paradigm is also a belief. We can say that our system of beliefs is our "system of paradigms."

What I am trying to demonstrate is how difficult it is nowadays to see something that is obvious, because of our system of beliefs/paradigms. We are blind to what is obvious unless we make a commitment to ourselves to be open-minded about learning *how to think*. The advantage now is that we have identified why we refuse to change. We now know that the rejection of new ideas, as beliefs or paradigms, is not entirely our conscious fault. It is not due to negligence, but to ignorance of some strange effect identified by scientists that, once we learn about it, we can decide to use our unlimited freedom of choice to liberate ourselves from its influence. How? By simply deciding to learn and unlearn. There are obstacles. It is not easy. But it is not impossible either.

To improve our knowledge, we need to fight this strange effect. We can choose not to let it affect us. We are empowered to do so because we have the faculties: we are fully equipped to do anything we want. We can also choose to resist the pressure of individuals and organizations interested in keeping people knowing only what to think instead of allowing them to find their own free way of thinking by themselves, practicing their own natural abilities to choose anew the belief they prefer, the belief that makes more sense to their inner knowledge. Each one of us is responsible for defining, developing and raising our own consciousness through our own thoughts, to become more and more conscious of what is true.

Remember: truth will make us free, because it is the only real "how to think"! It is fantastic to know that we are spiritual beings having human experiences, that we are free to control and decide our thoughts, that we determine and define our feelings, our emotions and our life in general through the way we think and interpret our world. And then, if we seriously take responsibility for our thoughts, using our unlimited freedom, learning as much as we can and changing accordingly, we grow to know how to think. What a concept!

We are entirely free to create our own search-for-meaning system, decide an effective *un*learning process for all those beliefs we want to discard, and simultaneously adopt any new paradigm that better agrees with our need for beliefs we feel and know with certainty are the right ones— the truth! Once you get yourself into the mind-changing frame, nothing will keep you from growing, however slowly. Always remember that your now expanded consciousness will never return to previous levels. For instance, learning how to think is something like being trained to use your new computer without being told what to use it for. You are free to use it for whatever pleases you; the important thing is you learned how to use it.

Following the same thought, we must change and allow ourselves to accept any idea that can help us to learn *how to think*, to liberate ourselves from the *what to think* we learned. Now let us go back to the lists on pages 1–6. And let us look at them in the light of the truth we glimpsed about paradigm shifts and the way we can be misled by what we have learned. We also must provide this information to future generations, because we have no right to impose limitations on them by telling them only what to think. They also need to be liberated to use their freedom to learn *how* to think, and we can surely help with that. As Stephen R. Covey quotes in his book *Principle-Centered Leadership*, "Give a man a fish and you feed him for a day; teach him how to fish and you feed him for a lifetime."

Learning how to think is to lead yourself to know, and knowledge unfolds from within when it provides wisdom. Learning how to think is also a way to become expert at healthy thinking, to obtain healthier responses from both your inner Self and your outer environment. Knowing how to think is, then, *the mastery of right living.*

The crisis created by "knowing" things that are *not* true is then solved by the utilization of our unlimited freedom, making the decision to claim our right to know the truths of life and to start collecting information that will better serve our need of improved understanding. We can change for the better. We deserve to enjoy life, not just to get through it with no clear understanding, suffering the undesirable effects of untrue "knowledge." We must approach with courage the missing piece that will allow us to close the gap created by the lack of right information, leading ourselves to also make a work of art out of our lives. For we are also responsible for defining, through our thoughts, our conscious awareness of the here and now—the only place and time where and when we are alive.

3

The Here and Now

THE whole story begins with the creation of the universe. It was formed as the outcome of a vast explosion known as the Big Bang. It is a well-accepted scientific theory that when the explosion occurred, some 13 to 18 billion years ago, time and space were created. The concept of time as we know it could be defined as the perceived delay that events use to happen, and the concept of space as the perceived room or space within the universe, occupied or not.

The universe contains theoretically some 100 billion galaxies. Our solar system occupies space in one of the spirals of the Milky Way galaxy, which contains at least 200 billion stars, of which our sun is one of the smaller. Planet Earth occupies space as the third planet of the solar system, after Mercury and Venus. We, as physical beings, occupy space on Earth at one specific time—the time that the only moment we are alive takes to manifest. Within this context, it is important to have an idea about where and when we are alive. The answer is: within the *Here and Now*, even if we were on another planet, or within another universe (if there is more than one).

We must define our lives in terms of time and space because we are having a human experience, a physical experience that appears to be limited by these two concepts.

It is limited by time because—according to the measuring system of seconds, minutes, hours, days, weeks, months, years, centuries, eons of time that we humans have established—we do not last as a physical expression forever. We may live more or less one hundred years, provided we take good care of our bodies. And our physical experience is limited by space because we cannot be in many places at the same time. We can be in only one place (here) at one portion of time (now).

Of course, we can be in a place, one moment after the other, or return to be there in another moment, immediately or long after the moment when we were in it— apparently the same location, never the same moment, never again the same now; and, despite the fact that it may sound contradictory, the place is not exactly the same in another moment, another now, because the *place* also changes. The atomic particles of the previous here will assume different conditions every moment. *The here is never the same from one moment to another.*

Only in the now can we remember the previous locations and moments in which we were alive. We call them the past. Also, only in the present moment do we expect to be alive in the coming heres and nows, which we identify as the future—although it does not exist for us yet. The future will exist for us only when it becomes a now— just when it ceases to be the future. It is the moment that has never been lived, because there is no future at any time or at any moment except in our perception. Similarly, there is no past at any moment—just in our collective or individual memories, or in the registration of events made in archives.

Because we are always in the now and this is all we have, if we have a pain that lasts several hours, it is lasting through a sequence of places and moments, because the pain is a continuous effect that transcends one *here and now* after the other. We could die in the third *here and now* after the pain started and the pain would not continue to be experienced; but since we continue to be alive, we keep on experiencing it. When the pain ceases for any reason, we will not perceive it in the next *here and now*, or it might gradually cease through several *heres* and *nows* until it disappears.

We may have long-lasting sensations through time and space: negative, as anger or physical pain; or positive, as love or physical comfort. But we live in only one *here and now* at a time. In the previous *here and now* we *were* living, and in the next we *might be* living; but the previous is gone and the next has not yet arrived.

If you would like to have a closer idea of one *here and now*, all you have to do is to take one of the pictures that you keep of yourself and observe how a *here and now* was trapped in the picture, frozen in time and space. In case you even remember how you were feeling when the picture was taken, and for a moment you feel the same again, you will confirm that the same feeling is occurring in a different moment and a different place—a different *here and now*.

If we are not enjoying life, taking advantage of the only *here and now* where we always are, we are wasting it! It will never be recovered. It becomes a portion of real physical experience of which we were not consciously aware, because we were not consciously benefiting from it by enjoying it!

When we realize that through our thinking we decide all of our feelings and our emotions, that we have the power to control them and that we can at any time decide how and what we want to feel, it is easy to conclude that we also decide how peaceful and happy we can be in any place and moment, despite the effort it might take to develop the necessary ability to achieve this wonderful outcome.

The reason why we need a redefinition of our lives in terms of time and space is not only to understand this fact, but also to prevent the wasting of more precious moments of our human experience in the only space and time where and when it happens to manifest.

Once we know where and when we are—never before or after the *here and now*—we need to clean it, to sanitize that *here and now* in which we always are. It might be contaminated by negative memories from the past or by fear for the future. If you were asked, "*Where* are you alive?" and you wanted to give accurate reply, you might answer, "*Here*; always *here*." And if you were asked, "*When* are you alive?" you might also answer, "*Now*; always *now*," without contradicting any point of view.

For example, if you were born on September 8, 1965, from that day to now you have lived a portion of time that is your human past. *This very moment* and *this very place* in which you are reading these lines, is the *here and now*. And the portion of time from this moment to the day you die physically will be your human future.

However, your experience in the present becomes severely affected when you remember your wrongdoings, when you feel guilt or shame, or if you remember others' wrongdoings that affected you, because you feel anger for mentally resenting the pain experienced. Both guilt and anger weigh you down, depress you. But since the past is gone, and is gone for good, and we cannot change that, the solution is *forgiveness*—which we shall explore in Chapter Six. Similarly, as will be confirmed in a subsequent chapter, your *here and now* is affected also when you develop fear that your future might not be as good as you expect. You then start developing anxiety. The solution is faith, self-reliance—reliance on the God within.

The *here and now* has no past and no future; it is independent of these. Only conceptually does it come from the past and project to the future. It is neither the past nor the future, but some argue that a very tenuous connection exists conceptually. Your *here and now* and my *here and now* are one and the same. Our *here and now* is also eternity! However, from the physical point of view it is perceived and interpreted as a "parenthesis in eternity." This is the idea of the *here and now*. And this is all there is for us human beings in relation to where and when we are alive, in relation to defining our lives in terms of time and space, in relation to something important to become consciously aware of.

Let's examine this. Imagine for a moment standing in the middle of a tile floor and placing yourself on one tile. In linear time you may now perceive the tile in front of you to be the future and the tile behind you the past. Now close your eyes, allowing your consciousness to become aware of the physical experience of a *here and now* represented by the tiles and think of the vastness of the universe of which we are all a part. Think about the place where, and the only moment in which, we are occupying it!

Did you feel something? Did you experience eternity for just a glimpse of time? I use this simple practice, this easy visualization, when I start meditation. It helps me to become aware of the Allness and the Oneness of God. I picture myself floating in eternity.

The *here and now* is all we have in life. You could be a billionaire, but if you are not enjoying your vast wealth within the *here and now* (as you are alive one instant and you die the next), your fortune is entirely worthless. It will go *to others*, not *with you*. You will not have another chance to use it. So use the *here and now*. Decide to be happy in it. Do not waste a single *here and now*, because it is irreplaceable.

You can do it with or without financial fortune, which has no bearing on your happiness. You might argue that you can be happier *with* the money, but I can tell you it is solely because you learned to interpret life as happy only if it comes with money. The fact of the matter is, money isn't worth wasting your *here and now* on! The *here and now* itself is your life's magnificent gift—your precious present.

On the other hand, it is good to learn—or, if you already know, to remember—that happiness is entirely free, especially for those who learn to achieve peace in the present and to define direction and meaning for their lives. I am not disparaging the experience of having money. I know it is good and useful to have money. I like it. I enjoy it. There is nothing wrong with that. But it is a fact that money is not a prerequisite for happiness!

All your fortune, your real and authentic fortune, is the *here and now*. It is the moment in which you are living—and it is not waiting for you to decide to enjoy it. Either you enjoy it or you lose it forever, in which case you will have wasted it! This is a physical aspect of our human experience. If we do not enjoy the *here and now*, it will not wait for us. It will not come again. *It will be gone forever.*

4

_____

Feelings and Emotions

Now let's talk about feelings and emotions. You now know that these two are your responsibility (your response-ability, no one else's!). If you do not develop or increase your ability to respond, making the changes in your life that you identify as crucial to making you response-able to yourself, to your loved ones and to others, you are severely reducing your chances of improvement.

Do you realize that only in the _here and now_ can you love? feel? hug? kiss? You _can_ decide. You _can_ be happy. Also in the _here and now_, using your freedom of choice, you can hate, you can choose not to decide, you can have all the negative emotions you want and be as unhappy as you wish.

If I asked you, "How do you wish to spend the next _here and now_—feeling well or feeling miserable?" I am sure you would reply, "Feeling well; at peace." You would not consciously choose to feel miserable. (Or would you?) So if you like wellness and peace, why have you had some rough patches in this lifetime? (It's okay. You probably did not have most of the information provided in this book!)

Discussing this subject with an audience in order to test how expert we have become at suffering unnecessarily, I

asked for a show of hands from those who could effortlessly make themselves feel unhappy. I suggested remembering a negative event from their past or thinking about
a few related to their future or interpreting in a negative
way what was going on in their lives at that very moment.

The entire audience raised their hands!

Then I asked for a show of hands from those who could
effortlessly make themselves *happy* by enjoying what was
going on in that very moment, with major emphasis on
being consciously aware of: 1. the fact that they were spiritual beings having temporary human experiences, and
2. their life conditions and their freedom to make any interpretation of them they wished.

No hands went up. The justification was almost uni-
form. No one had yet learned how to do it. However, they
all agreed that we can become happy by the mere awareness of our being. Everybody understood the intention of
the test. Each of the participants recognized that it was
possible and "right" to make a decision to enjoy life. But
all pleaded a lack of practice and a lack of ability to enjoy, which resulted from a lifetime spent adopting wrong
beliefs.

Yes, there is a need for change. *You can change any
time you so decide*. And you can receive all the support
you need from your self, your inner Self. God does indeed
help those who decide to help themselves. But now you
are in a quandary, for you have come to realize that you
have no excuse for ever feeling unhappy. There is no excuse, either, for your not taking active responsibility for
your life in order to create the happiness that is your birth-
right, because nothing and no one is keeping you from it,
except you!—and probably because of the paradigm effect. Happiness is for everybody. The Dalai Lama says:
"The very purpose of our life is happiness."

Your family status, your work position and/or conditions, or your social environment, are not excuses either. But if you opt for happiness, any unfavorable family, work or social conditions begin to improve immediately As you change from within, everything around you starts changing, simply because the joy for life comes from within, not from outside.

Working on increasing your abilities to respond better to yourself and others is the next best choice you can make after opting for happiness. You will not only improve the quality of your relationship with your family and your community, but you will also perform better at work and enjoy not only the satisfaction, but also the rewards that come with a job done well.

You are clear by now that whatever may be happening in the *here and now* can be faced and solved by you, or enjoyed by you. You no longer need to suffer unnecessarily because of past events or fears about the future. In the present, apart from physical injury, nothing can affect you, because by learning *how* to think, you also learn how to decide your interpretations of all the external conditions, effects and situations.

A sense of wellness in the *here and now* means only absence of pain—pain that is mainly produced by self-inflicted sentiments of guilt, anger or fear. The absence of pain makes room for peace; and peace provides plenty of room for happiness.

Change is not easy; understanding and then internalizing all these facts is not easy. It requires getting involved in spiritual activities or finding a spiritual environment that will suport your efforts towards improvement. I suggest that you will perhaps want consciously to define and then select the spiritual environment that will help you the most with your quest.

Trying to live this human experience without understanding that we are spiritual beings is like ignoring our need for air. You may deny that you are a spiritual being, but that does not change the fact that you are. Accepting it leads you immediately to realize that you are an expression of God, a son or a daughter of God, a creation of God, a manifestation of God, with no fewer rights than anyone else; because God does not differentiate among humans as we humans tend to do out of ignorance. You will immediately realize that God is within you, that you carry with you this Power greater than the physical you, greater than all of us, willing at all times to be your counselor and your provider if you only ask.

It is imperative that you become involved in spiritual activities, by yourself or with other people, that support your decision of changing in order to have a better life, a new way of living without unnecessary suffering; for no suffering is necessary. Still, we often fail to see the need for making the changes in our lives that will improve them unless severe pain compels us to do so. We are so accustomed to what we have learned!

Since we are spiritual beings having a human experience, an experience that becomes synthesized in the *here and now*, we need spiritual support for the comprehension of our human manifestation. When we are not happy, it is because we are keeping ourselves away from physical consciousness and spiritual awareness of the wonderful experience that life is.

We become absorbed by irrelevant, temporary life conditions that we have learned to interpret as "problems." These conditions might always exist; but if you have spiritual understanding, you know there are no such things as "problems." So-called problems are only the outcome of our way of thinking, of the kind of beliefs we hold and, consequently, of the way we interpret our temporary life conditions. The experience of these conditions will be gone along with the moment we lived in which they were perceived and interpreted as "problems"—another extinct *here and now*. Another vanished set of appearances!

Of course, when we have pain—a toothache for example—we cannot very easily deny it. We cannot ignore it; we cannot pretend not to have it. We need to deal with it as best we can in that moment, with solutions such as taking a pain-killer or going to the dentist. And once the pain is over, we will do what is necessary to avoid repeating the experience.

Notice the difference: In the present you can change conditions. You would say that you can solve "problems," but let me insist that there are only *conditions interpreted by you as "problems."* In the present you can react and change yourself and many of the external conditions that surround you. You cannot change the past—just your interpretation of it. You also cannot create the future in the present. You can only plan for it, develop a vision of what you want for it—and do, in the *here and now*, exactly what may contribute to arriving at your vision and attaining it.

When you come to understand the origins of life in its multiple expressions and become aware of the wonderful design of the universe, its contents and its story of how we humans came to exist on this small planet Earth, you will conclude that we are not the result of a simple biological phenomenon, but rather the product of a divine and precise plan involving the most wondrous projection of evolution, with a great purpose. It is then that you find yourself in awe! There is a Great Intelligence projecting Its thoughts through all the universe, which is Its body. All of us are equally small "branches" of this great Intelligence. Such convictions wonderfully support your intellectual understanding, your emotional stability, and your physical response to life in this beautiful environment that we have been given.

The *here and now* is an expression often used by poets and writers and is loved by many, especially romantics. However, the *here and now* is something that goes far beyond the common understanding of it. It is all we have, and we can always enjoy it. We immediately tend to suffer when there is lack of *here-and-nowness*, when we are not aware of what is going on in the precise *here and now* in which we are.

5

Total Freedom

W E can do the right thing in the *here and now* or do exactly the wrong thing (in spite of consequences) because of our total freedom as spiritual beings manifesting as humans. What is the right or the wrong thing to do or not to do? The right thing is never to violate the natural laws or principles of the Universe, because we will have to face the consequences.

In the same vein, we must respect human laws, even if we do not agree with them. If you do not agree with some human legislation, do something practical to promote a change of it, but do not violate it. Regardless of whether the violaton involves fines or penalties, do not violate any human law, because you do not have the enforcing power and you might be risking unnecessary suffering. Do not violate it either, if *you* have the enforcement obligation—because that would be deceitful. Rather, look for ways to improve the legislation. We need no violation of any law to have a happy and satisfactory human experience. What we *do* need is careful observance of Universal Laws, the natural laws or principles of the universe.

Freedom entails our inherent right to choose. You can choose the *what*, *why*, *where*, *who*, *when* and the *how*. And if you choose wrong, you are free to change any time, to choose again. Our freedom has no limits. Freedom is free. Freedom is volition in action.

Any need for changes in attitude or behavior in a personal, work or business relationship can be easily discerned. Accurate information or proper training might be called for. Still, as you probably have already proven, individuals will end up doing as they wish. They will use their freedom to change for the better or for the worse, or not to change at all. What if they do not change for the better? In this case you can always use your freedom to make changes yourself.

You can change partners, relinquish your job, fire your associate, deal with a different supplier, look for a different customer, move to another location or change your interpretation about the particular condition. We are all free at all times. By making no change at all, you are using your freedom too. You are freely deciding *not* to make any change. This is why it is useless to complain about any life experience.

There is need to interpret individual freedom to the best possible extent, just as in business when we come to understand the market and its inherent spontaneous freedom. We can experience a great manifestation of freedom, for example, when we allow a real market economy to manifest, without government intervention, monopolies, privileges or foreign forces to limit the free exchange of the participating products or services. Knowledgeable businesspersons understand that violations of natural market laws will make the violator pay with and through the consequences.

Individuals who have learned *how* to think have no desire to violate any law or principle. They demonstrate healthy thinking that recognizes others as spiritual beings who also are going through a human experience and who also are free to choose. It is here that the only difference is manifested between individuals who have learned *how* to think and those who have lived with the *what*-to-think that they learned. The former knows of his or her condition as a spiritual being and knows how to use his or her limitless faculties. The latter, unaware of these gifts, cannot use them before committing to the radical change that has been proposed.

How can you get to higher levels of living if you do not get the basics? The very first foundation is peace in the *here and now*. That is why we need to focus on the *here and now* and why we need to learn *how* to think instead of keeping ourselves thinking only the "whats" that we learned to think. We must seriously challenge our current beliefs. We must come to understand that we are one with the Universal Creative Intelligence, because we are a product of It.

If we become aware that this Intelligence manifests through us, as us, and therefore *is* us, I can assure you that, unless you make a mistake in the process, you will be creating the foundation for the first and most important requirement of your development: peace! The peace you have always desired has forever been in your hands, but you never knew it . . . until now.

I am going to share with you the method for attaining peace first. Then comes happiness, followed by enthusiasm—and then the joy of life. Remember: you need only decide to begin to learn *how* to think, knowing that you can—because you are pure Universal Intelligence.

If you ask yourself what kind of stuff are you made of, Deepak Chopra might tell you that you are energy and information. Both are manifestations of the Creative Intelligence that made the entire universe and everything in it. We are, then, that Intelligence in both our physical vehicle and our Inner Self! Is there anything else?

If you do not buy all of these ideas, still it will suffice if you just embrace, for now, the importance of knowing *how* to think instead of knowing only *what* to think. By knowing how to think, you will sooner or later reach the conclusions presented here. In fact, all this information has been revealed in one way or another in countless other books and information media by many poeple. What I am offering is an interpretation of many of these as well as some experiences that can be of vital use to you.

I do not have a secret formula for happiness to give you, because it is not secret. The ''formula,'' as such, is openly available to all. I wouldn't want this formula to be available only to the fortunate few who already know it and who are already happy: all those who intuitively or through research have discovered these ideas themselves and have shared them in the many books I have read, and all those clever enough not to have learned many of the existing wrong beliefs.

Rather, I want to see this formula become as popular and as easily used as is our current practice of blaming others for how we act and feel! When we learn the truth of our relationship with God and we come to understand that God is within us—not outside, as we were erroneously told—we come to understand why we shall ''live'' forever, why we shall not ''die.''

This is because God does not die—because God is Eternity. I believe that we, as individual spiritual entities created in the image and likeness of God, move from one expression of life to another in a constant evolution and in a constant expansion of our individual awareness, just as the whole expansive universe does.

Knowing this, we shall have no more fear—which will then be a disused emotion. We shall begin to understand that we are merely having a tour on planet Earth—a short round trip—and that the purpose of our human experience is primarily to master our freedom in the *here and now*. Then, when the current *here and now* is cleansed of impurities and contamination, when we have begun to clearly comprehend our Higher Inner Self, we shall have grown in spiritual understanding to such a degree that we shall truly experience God—which is the main purpose of all!

When we begin to understand that the *here and now* is always one moment at a time, and all the time there is, and that we decide how and what we want to feel within it, we become conscious of the God within us and finally aware, too, that we all are within God as one with God. We begin to raise and expand our consciousness to higher levels, in a marvelous intensity that will take us to dimensions of higher spiritual manifestations accumulating experience that will make us, as individual spiritual entities, ever more joyful and useful.

Much of the satisfaction in our life comes from the discovery that there is no inherent reality to suffering—that suffering results only from our adopted negative beliefs and the learned negative ways of interpreting external conditions and events. Also, much of that satisfaction is in the remarkable fact that we are totally free to use new ways of interpreting from now on. It is also very rewarding to discover that our loved ones are not responsible for making us suffer, as we used to believe. Realizing that the ''suffering'' was our chosen reaction to the way we used to interpret external events or conditions, we now absolve our loved ones of the blame we used to put on them.

The experiences that we remember as negative, that are

seemingly keeping us from being happy, are just an illusion. Why? Because they *are not any more*. They are not happening any more. What remains is the memory of them, and this is subject to interpretation. Yes, *you can change the past* by changing the interpretation of the event you are remembering. You do not change the *event*, because it *is not* any more. You simply change the *interpretation* of it and, consequently, the effect of the previous interpretation.

We have no true limitations on our happiness, even if we happen to be physically impaired. We can be happy in any circumstance, because happiness springs from being at peace with ourselves, the world and the Universe, and from having the inner certainty that we are all Children of God and are responsibly using our unlimited freedom.

As we have observed, our life on this planet is a sequence of *nows* in a sequence of *heres*. You will always be somewhere at one moment. This is all you have for a life: the moment that you are alive in the place where you are alive, wherever you might be.

Always remember, in the pure sense of *having*, that this is all that you have, all that you own and all that you will ever have: the eternal *here and now*! We have to realize that lamenting what we do not have in the moment we are alive, whatever the object of our lamentation may be, is a waste of all that we have: *this very precious present*.

We can first of all enjoy what we have while doing whatever we understand we must to get what we are missing. Are we not totally free? It is not really intelligent to waste any moment feeling badly when we know we are free to decide *how we want to feel*. You can give yourself all the peace you want, all the happiness you want—or all the turmoil and unhappiness you want.

Nobody else can give you any peace or any happiness.

You have freedom of choice; but lest you forget that all the good that is not given gets wasted, you should decide right now to give yourself the very best and stop wasting all the good that you are not presently giving to yourself. You can take full responsibility for anything you experience, from this *here and now* on. Do not quit too soon after the first failure—or after the first success. And if you choose unhappiness, at least do it conscious of the fact that you are freely selecting it!

Our usual greeting to another is, "How are you?" and we get answers such as "I feel lousy!" or "I feel great!" Did you notice that the question was: "How *are* you?" not: "How do you *feel*?" After an accident a man who was asked "How are you?" replied, "I am in pretty bad shape. My leg is trapped between two pieces of metal, I can see a piece of my leg bone protruding through the skin, but I feel great for being alive. All around me is death!" Wouldn't you agree he really answered the question?

Recently a minister told about two persons who took the same train to go to the same destination. One was going from window to window enjoying the landscape, talking to the other passengers and making comments on the joys of train travel. The other stayed in his seat and sulked all the way. It's the same with life. How do you prefer to live it? What kind of tourist are you on this planet? Are you enjoying the tour?

You are probably familiar with the little prayer *"God, grant me the Serenity to accept the things I cannot change, the Courage to change the things I can, and the Wisdom to know the difference."* I'm sure you'll agree that it is a very humane prayer. Venturing to understand its deep meaning, I would suggest that:

1. With the first sentence, we are asking for the ability to accept (a) other individuals (spouses, relatives, friends, peers) exactly as they are, exactly as they behave, because we cannot change them—because they have their own freedom too, (b) things like the weather, geography, political and economic systems as well as other conditions that we cannot change, and (c) our past, with all its contents, because we also cannot change that.

2. With the second sentence we are asking for the courage to make changes where it is possible to make them. We might need to make changes in ourselves. As we have learned, we can make changes in ourselves any time we want, but we cannot change other individuals, because they have their own freedom and consequently their own choice. They can change themselves, individually. However, we can influence their lives with our prayers, if they consent. But you now know that the only corner in the entire Universe where you can make real changes is in yourself.

We do not have to be like our parents or anyone else in the world, unless we unequivocally decide to be so. We do not have to do the same thing as anyone else and, as a consequence, have the same limitations, the same diseases. We decide our human experience with our thinking, and because of this, we can be as different as we may want to be from everybody else.

Besides making changes in ourselves, we can also change or influence many external things, provided we do not waste our time trying to change another person, and as long as we violate no principle or law. To make the desired changes, we must have the courage to take action. All we need to decide is the "what," and have a good satisfactory "why," in order to start taking action and to start witnessing how the necessary resources to accomplish our goal will naturally come to us, together with the bravery that God will be granting us.

3. The third sentence addresses our need to know the difference between something we would like to change but cannot (for example, other poeple, some external conditions, the past) and something we perceive as unchangeable but that can be changed at any time with just a little decisiveness (for example, ourselves, many external things, our fears for the future). The knowledge might be in us, but not the wisdom to understand the difference.

Allow me to give you an example recently shared with me, in which a woman could not move from her bed because of her extreme overweight. She had gotten serenity and rest by accepting what she felt she could not change —her overweight condition. There is lacking here that knowledge which produces wisdom, because her condition *can* be changed. She simply ignores it or else she unconsciously does not want to change it. In any case, she is not showing any wisdom. This is why getting to know *how* to think will allow us to differentiate among the various kinds of knowledge; for we may even be getting too much knowledge—but not the kind that produces wisdom.

The wisdom of knowing the difference makes all the difference: (a) accepting others the way they decide to be, without trying to force changes on them, but providing enough accurate information to enable them to use their understanding and their freedom to make the changes they desire for their own betterment, and (b) accepting the past with all its contents.

6

The Past and Forgiveness

I F we consider the day we were born up to this present moment as our past, we shall have to understand that this past exists only in our memory, because all the events that happened in it, including the most recent one, are gone. They remain only in our memory. Our memory in the *here and now* is telling us, as we go on remembering, that we did good, positive things *in the past*. It is also telling us that others also did good, positive things *in the past*. In the same sense, we remember some of our actions as wrongdoings, which are our negatives *in the past*. We also remember some actions others did that we consider bad actions, and we see them as their negatives *in the past*. Actually, that's all the past is: *memories of what happened*.

In this moment, in the *here and now*, if we remember the good things, the positives (ours and others'), we shall probably smile and feel a sense of well-being. However, if we remember our negatives—our actions interpreted as wrongdoings—we shall have a sense of guilt or shame (or both) despite the fact that these actions are not happening any more.

If now we remember others' negative actions toward us, we shall have a sensation of anger, because we are resenting the hurt received, interpreted by us as caused by them

—and we become angry again. These actions are not happening any more, but we are resenting them as much as, and sometimes more than, when they happened.

Awareness of the *here and now* tells us that any event in the past is *not* happening any more; and anyway, if something similar were happening, it would be a different event from that in the past. Feeling guilty, sorry or ashamed when you remember your wrongdoings, or feeling angry over having been hurt by others, prevents your achieving peace in the *here and now*. Feeling guilt or anger does not evoke a sense of peace.

You can miss the peace you would like to have in the *here and now* simply by resenting negatives from the past. Think instead that, because they are in the past, they are already gone. They do not exist any more. They are not happening any more. You are in the *here and now*, and that excludes the past. Any negatives could have seemed real when they were happening; but they are happening no more. Now they are only memories. And there are better things to do with which you can have pleasure in the *here and now*.

We need somehow to insist that we, as human beings, are only *temporarily* that—human beings, physical beings. On a *permanent* basis, we are spiritual beings coming from eternity and going back to it—to other experiences, in other worlds, in other dimensions. We are only having this human experience in "between," synthesized only in one moment (now) and in one place (here). The past exists only in our memory, and the future only in our creative imagination.

The best thing to do is to dwell in the *here and now* and not be concerned with, or (most especially) suffer for, events that already have vanished. Of course, our memory has a purpose. It helps us to remember mistakes made and their consequences so we can avoid them. They help us to learn. When I suggest dwelling in our present moment, I mean deciding to be consciously aware of the *here and now* **in the here and now**—to be consciously aware of our life in the only moment in which it occurs, but using the lessons learned from the past.

Similarly, it is unproductive to waste any *here and now* remembering good things that happened in the past when we can be enjoying what is happening now—those unlimited possibilites the current moment has to offer. We can be consciously aware of so many wonderful things, such as the taste of food, the absence of extreme temperatures, a beautiful piece of music, the flower's scent, the creativity of what we are doing—so many good things that are not perceived and enjoyed because we are not focused on the *here and now*.

Sometimes we allow our thoughts to be completely absorbed by the past. We cling to the past. Many of us do. You have heard expressions like "How good things used to be when I was young!" or "Too bad things change!" and "I'd rather live with my memories!" These come from persons who are living in the past and not enjoying the present. They have not yet developed the ability of responding better to themselves in the now. They have not made the right changes, although change swirls all about them.

It's even worse when you remember negatives, because by doing this you lose any sense of well-being you may have had, unless you have consciously reconciled yourself with the past through the use of forgiveness, that magnificent tool for peace. In any case, one loses the precious *here and now* because it gets occupied with thoughts about the past or the future. Remembering negatives produces a sense of guilt or a sense of anger and, in any case, a sense of depression.

Depression in this case is the effect of bringing to the *here and now* negative memories from the past—or what you *consider* negative memories because of the way you learned to interpret some past events. Besides forgiving, you might also need to change your interpretation of "negative." You might very well see your memories as *your record of lessons* to which you can refer time and again to identify what you do not wish to repeat or to expose yourself to.

You can identify the good in the negative experience, the good from which you can benefit as from a lesson that might have contributed to your making better decisions for a much better life. This is growth! For we are reaching maturity when we begin to really expand our consciousness.

We must stop opposing ourselves, being against ourselves. We must reconcile ourselves with the past. We must stop confirming that we are our own worst enemies. Again, the key to this is forgiveness. There is no better way. We can reconcile our lives with the past and recognize its events as some of those things we cannot change. We can recognize that they have already happened; and, because they have happened, they are unchangeable.

I recently heard the comment "Even God does not want to change the past!" Of course, there is no purpose in erasing the lessons of this school called life. If we deny the existence of a lesson, it is because we do not want to recognize the fact that there are always lessons and that there always will be so long as our physical experiences last—especially those lessons that repeat themselves time and again until we finally decide to learn them.

Our first step is to work on anger caused by resentment over hurts received, because we may at any time relinquish our resentments. Forgiving others for what they did will allow us to develop the ability to forgive ourselves for our guilt, the guilt we perceive as making us suffer in the *here and now*.

There could be many ways to forgive, but let me suggest that you use the time immediately after a meditation session to do your forgiving. (In fact, I used several sessions, one for each individual or group of individuals that I wanted to forgive.) After a moment of stillness, with the image in mind of the individual or group and the aggression or offense that you want to forgive, say mentally or in a loud voice, "I forgive you for _____," and be specific! This declaration is for your benefit. Just do it and let go. You cannot forget, but you can release and then relax.

Forgiving does not mean approval of the actions that affected you. If we are able to forgive others in an authentic way, from within, we shall be able to forgive ourselves and recover the freedom and the peace we deserve to enjoy in the *here and now*—the freedom we lost because of ignorance. In other words, we shall be liberating ourselves for the use of our natural freedom to live peacefully. One of the themes of our principal prayer is: "And forgive us our offenses, as we have forgiven our offenders."

Forgiving ourselves means to see clearly our deliberate or unintentional errors and to make a list of those for which we have been feeling guilt. In the list we may include such unintentional errors as having only learned *what* to think instead of *how* to think; supporting false beliefs, doctrines, convictions, philosophies or practices.

In addition to forgiving someone, after the same or another meditation session, communicate to yourself, si-

lently or out loud: "I forgive myself for _____, consciously aware of the fact that God is in me, as me,
therefore *is* me." Then let go, releasing the past once and
for all. Forgiveness of the negative portion of the past
equals peace in the *here and now*; but additionally, it
means the liberation of the energy that you have been using to handle anger and guilt, using it in more fruitful
ways.

Of course, if you can personally ask the offended individual or individuals for forgiveness, or you can correct
anything that went wrong without causing additional
harm, this is obviously a better way to recover your peace.
However, if you think you might cause further harm,
refrain from approaching the offended party; but stop
suffering now for something that happened in the past and
that cannot be changed. Your current suffering will never
change the past. It will only affect your life in the now,
which is an unnecessary waste. If you forgive yourself,
you recover the portion of life in which you used to feel
guilty, ashamed or both. Of course, we shall remember,
we shall again have memories of negative past events; but
we shall not feel either the anger or the guilt—because we
have forgiven, and because we are therefore reconciled
with the past.

If we do not feel well yet, we shall feel better immediately after we remember that we have already forgiven.
It is not easy to change a life-pattern that has been with
us since the day we learned it until now, when we begin
to understand this process of change. If we consistently
remember that we have already forgiven, we shall achieve
the necessary reconciliation of our lives with the past, and
the past will not affect us any more. What a relief! What
a liberation!

We will not even waste more life remembering the good

times, because we shall be busy experiencing the *here and now*, enjoying what it has to offer: new and rich experiences of pure good life—not past memories or future chimeras. Forgiveness offers power. A broken heart that is able to forgive becomes empowered to go through life in peace. This in turn provides the platform on which happiness can be mounted in our life. Let's not forget that if we are not first at peace, we cannot be happy.

Unforgiveness only contributes to the experience of pain in the *here and now*, even if we are taking advantage of the hurt received or the hurt is much a part of our current life—as though we feared we might be nothing without "our" story of the hurt.

Sometimes we might think we have forgiven and we have not. We notice this because the effects of not forgiving keep coming back until we really forgive; but only you will know when this is happening to you.

We have spoken of forgiveness, but why do we need to forgive? The individuals who hurt us do not *deserve* to be forgiven; they *deserve* to be *punished*, right? And if we forgive, we might feel we are condoning their actions or making them feel better about what they did.

This is not true. We can and should keep the two ideas separate. We do not need to condone a debt, but we do need to forgive to attain peace within ourselves. Being unforgiving is the same as being against ourselves. By not forgiving, we are not affecting the aggressor or offender, who might not even realize the intensity of our anger; but because we decided to have this emotion after recalling the action we interpreted as aggression or offense, we upset only ourselves.

The alleged offender might even have died during the time we harbored the negative emotion that chews us up with anger and resentment. Resenting that hurt can create a greater pain than that caused while the actual aggression or offense was taking place. You see, by not forgiving, we affect only ourselves. We are not affecting the aggressor or offender in any way.

We do not deserve additional pain, additional hurt. We are free to use any resource to liberate ourselves from continuing unnecessary suffering for an aggression or offense that happened in the past. But by deciding not to forgive, we certainly choose to be against ourselves, whereas we could choose in favor of forgiveness. The important point for you is to recognize that the anger is in you—it is not in the aggressor or offender. You developed this anger for the aggression or offense received, but the anger does nothing to help you live and enjoy your life. You must forgive if you are still suffering.

It is not vengeance or retaliation that reconciles you with your past; it is forgiveness: because by forgiving, you are doing a favor to yourself—not necessarily to your aggressor or offender. The importance of forgiving is in getting rid of your constant resentment, which is causing anger one moment after another as you remember a past event that has already vanished and remains only in your memory.

Forgiving is important for your own sake, for your own health, and for your own well-being. You need to forgive even if you find a wrong uncondonable. Forgiving is cleansing your life; it is a catharsis, a depuration and a purification of it. If you forgive, you first have the benefit of having learned *how* to forgive; and then you produce the well-deserved peace of mind required to be happy. Remember that once you have successfully forgiven, you develop in practice the wonderful skill of forgiving, which you will use later to forgive yourself.

After forgiving, each new time that you remember the

event that affected you, you will also remember that you *have* forgiven, that the event is not happening any more and that you are already reconciled with its past manifestation. If this doesn't work, it could only be that you were not sincere at the time of forgiving. This could be the case. The solution: repeat the whole process until you feel the peace inside, then let go by mentally releasing it.

When something happened, you recognized the event as real for you. Now you recognize that it is one of the things you cannot change because it has already happened. You do not necessarily need to change the interpretation you made of that event when it took place, but you do need to forgive it. (You will have the opportunity to change the interpretation later on if you still want to.)

Suppose that you are affected by someone who cheated you financially and you lost thousands of dollars. I believe there are two lessons for you to benefit from, after anger subsides: you will take immediate steps to prevent additional financial loss if you can; and you might as well decide that you will never treat others similarly, not only from a sense of integrity, but because you now know what happens when someone is deceived in the same way.

This is defining your future attitude, thus your future behavior. Do you see the benefit? The things in the past that are producing anger now are not necessarily bad. They are in the past—not here any more. We are the ones who bring them here only to affect us, and this we do not need. Meanwhile, the originator of the event is probably not thinking about it any more; the originator has probably forgotten about us—but we are still keeping alive the past event, we are still giving strength to it, allowing ourselves to be affected. We can't even blame the originator for the current effect because we are affecting ourselves by not forgiving.

Going through life with anger is often like drinking small doses of poison. We are constantly poisoning our system. Even if we conclude that the aggressor or offender does not deserve our forgiveness, the truth is that *we* deserve it. We deserve to forgive and halt the poisoning, we deserve peace in the *here and now*.

Let's test the intensity of our forgiveness. If we now know that we have forgiven—if we think we did it in an authentic manner, from deep inside ourselves—we should then be able to see God in the forgiven being and to send love to him, to her or to them. *If you are able to send love, the memories of the offense will never again affect you.*

The purpose of forgiving is just to grant ourselves peace in the *here and now*. On the other hand, the purpose of being consciously aware that we are not separated from God, that we can trust God—the God in ourselves—is to eliminate anxiety for the future within ourselves and to also provide peace in the *here and now*.

This is key. This is the way to a happy life. You cannot be happy if you do not have peace first. You cannot be enthusiastic if you are not already happy; and finally, you cannot enjoy your life if you are not able to forgive and are not able to trust God.

7

The Future and Faith

Now let's talk about the future. In the future we have more or less the same features that we identified for the past. We imagine most of our future actions and the future actions of others as positive, especially those actions that will benefit us. These are the so-called dreams developed by a positive attitude toward life, and from them we should extract a clear vision for our future.

Unfortunately, many people have fear: fear that the good things they expect might not happen and fear that the things they do not want will come to be. They have fear either for the whole future or for only part of it; but *they have fear*. They develop an expectation of loss, an expectation of pain that can reach very real proportions, even though nothing has happened yet or, worse, never will happen sufficiently for these worriers to claim accuracy for their predictions. Fear about the development or nondevelopment of future events, in addition to exhausting energy, creates a paralyzing effect that prevents us from responding and inhibits us from being response-able.

With fear we imagine a future with negatives for ourselves and for others. These thoughts as expectations of loss, pain and suffering cause us to develop anxiety. And here we are, living in the *here and now* under the effects

of anger/guilt-induced depression or fear-generated anxiety, and sometimes both of these. They are a root cause
of much neurosis. This is why many people do not realize they are living outside of reality.

All the reality of our physical life is the *here and now*
because the past is gone and the future is not yet. The *here
and now* is real because it is where and when our human
manifestation is being experienced—the only place and the
only moment—the only reality from any point of view
within the physical world.

The past, real at the time, is like a mirage that has already vanished; and the future is an imagined illusion that
does not become true unless we experience it in the *here
and now*, which is all we have. Nothing from the past or
the future is actually real for us, except what is happening in the *here and now*. On the other hand, the only Reality in the Universe is God. If we are aware of all this, we
can build a positive future in the *here and now* by understanding that everything happens only within it.

You can plan for future *heres* and *nows* in the current
here and now, visualize them, and, if possible, develop a
clear version of your entire vision for the rest of your life.
You will be in your future what you are thinking now you
will be, because we are the product of our thoughts. You
will have in your future the good you now think and
visualize, or the bad you now fear. However, if you want
to have something different from what you fear, change
your mind, change your thinking, and you will be changing your life accordingly. If you wish to define your future, you may develop a vision of what you really want—
and you will get it!

Instead of being *pre*occupied about the future, be *occupied* now in planning for it. There is plenty of room for
our hopes and our dreams. In case you develop fear that

later becomes anxiety, use the only solution recognized by philosophers, religious leaders and professionals who assist individuals in solving their emotional problems. This solution is faith. Faith is the antidote for fear, indeed for any manifestation of anxiety. Faith produces authentic peace in the *here and now*! It is unfortunate to see how many people say they have faith but do not, much less know how to use it. And many do not even know how to *have* it.

Many say they have faith, but they do not expect to be successful in what they are planning to do. This is only proof that they do *not* have the faith they say they have. You cannot have *a little* faith, or *half* faith. Either you have faith or you do not. After all, you would not say that a woman was a *little* pregnant or *half* pregnant. A woman is pregnant or she is not. Either you believe in God or you do not.

It is true that faith sounds like something abstract, subjective, invisible. But everybody knows, or has seen, the results of faith; and these make it visible. Faith is the authentic, genuine, reliable inner feeling of certainty that we can use the power of God, the power of that omnipresent Universal Intelligence that is within us and, as us, *is* us.

We all remember those "great miracles" that happened in our lives—things we requested, sometimes in a moment of desperation, that became true without any logical explanation. We have forgotten those "miracles" because we could not explain how they happened. They happened, you may be assured, because of *faith*.

If we fear that God will not answer our prayers, it is because we learned to know fear better than we believe we know God or even ourselves. We are misusing our freedom by creating fear. Fear is no more than an imaginary competing power created by us, simply because we do not trust God or ourselves. It is only our imagination. Fear exists only as a concept, because it can be and is conceived. Fear is one of the wrong beliefs we learned—we were not born with it. Fear is not an entity; it is just an idea created by humankind; thus we should not have faith in it. But we *do*—because of a lack of trust in our divine reality, because of the wrong learned beliefs about God.

People fail to have or receive what they want because they cannot see that they are trusting fear more than they are trusting God. And what can this mentally created disconnectedness from God provide? It provides exactly what they fear! Fear is powerful because humans are powerful. Humans can empower their fear *or* they can put all their power in faith, trust and well-founded hope. There are not two powers, only one—the Oneness of God manifested in us humans because we exist within God, because God is all there is, because God is the Universe.

We must be careful that we do not, out of fear, misplace our faith in imaginary, nonexisting gods such as fear, astrology, card- or palm-readings. We sometimes want someone knowledgeable to tell us what to do with our future to save us the "inconvenience" of having to go through the process of defining it ourselves.

Why should you allow other individuals, with less knowledge about you than you have, to guide you and define your future? Have you forgotten it is *your life* we are talking about and the fact that you have a choice? Is it possible that you lost, for some reason, your faith in God, the faith you had when you were born? Is it possible that you have forgotten your divine origin because you have allowed yourself to be absorbed by the modern, technological age to the point where you no longer believe in God? *Have you forgotten God?*

I believe that when we come to this world and are exposed to the current crop of wrong beliefs, we end up forgetting a lot of information that was with us as the spiritual beings we are. We then need to regain the spiritual awareness we lost. Arianna Huffington, in her book *The Fourth Instinct*, tells the following story, which most appropriately illustrates this matter:

Radio commentator Gil Gross once reported on the young parents who brought home a new baby brother to his four-year-old sister. The little girl immediately wanted to be left alone with him, but the parents were fearful. They had heard of jealous children hitting new siblings and didn't want the baby hurt.

"Why do you want to be alone with him?" they asked. "What are you going to do?"

"Nothing," the little girl said; "I just want to be alone with him."

But the parents weren't comfortable and so the little girl heard "no, no" and "not yet" day after day.

After one week of incessant entreaties, the parents finally gave in. There was an intercom in the baby's room. They would listen. If they heard crying, they could rush in and snatch up the baby.

So the little girl went in, alone. She walked quietly to the crib where her baby brother slept. Then, after a minute, over the intercom, the parents heard her plead, "Tell me about God. I'm forgetting."*

I sincerely hope one day we shall be able to assist newcomers to this world in not forgetting God, not getting disconnected, as almost all of us up to now have become!

If you are not getting the happiness you deserve, check carefully. You might have forgotten God, or you might

*Arianna Huffington, *The Fourth Instinct: The Call of the Soul* (New York: Simon & Schuster, 1994), pp. 135–36.

have been worshiping the wrong one. Certainly you would be better off making a paradigm shift by moving your faith back to the real God and releasing your belief in a fake. I am overwhelmed watching the huge number of people who express the need for believing in something different, something reliable, because they do not trust the idea of a god outside them, especially a vindictive, punishing one. They are not conscious that the real God is within each of us. It is so true that, when they learn it, they accept it intuitively, willingly—as if they had known it all the time.

They express the need to believe in some power strong enough to support them, to sustain them in regaining control of their lives. They have lost control over their lives because they do not know *how* to think; they only learned *what* to think—the limited and much-distorted, inherited information that allows them to believe in anything, including fear, before trusting God. These imaginary gods do not have any power. Again, it is *you* who empower them. God is in you; thus *you have the power*.

You were granted total freedom, which you are misusing by relying on false powers. You can use that power properly by placing your faith in *you*, in your inner voice, in the God within you that, as you, *is* you! Isn't that fantastic—but credible and believable?

There is only One Universal God that is within and around all human beings, with no distinction of color or social, financial or political conditions. God created you entirely free. You can use that freedom to deny the truth that God is in you, but your denial does not change that truth. Until you freely accept it, you have been denying it! Experiencing the denial is a great lesson. It is how we learn. The freedom you use to create imaginary gods and to misplace your faith is the same freedom you can use to reconnect yourself with your inner Self and to redirect your faith.

Being a spiritual being that is having human experiences does not mean that you as a human will automatically express spiritual conviction. You need to recover your natural sense of connectedness, lost because as humans we learn "separation" instead. This happens to a large number of us.

Now take a look at the consequences. You may have lost control of your life if you are not happy, if you drink, smoke, eat or gamble in excess, or use drugs or depend on an astrology wizard, a palm- or card-reader, or even if you work in excess. You have also lost control of your life if you live in depression and/or anxiety.

If you are not happy, you are hiding yourself from your own life, from the fantastic joy that represents having this human experience in peace with yourself and with the world. Suffering is not necessary. All you need is to regain control over your life by learning *how to think*. If you know how to think, it means that you have a clear and reliable basis for regaining your natural sense of connectedness and for defining your life in the future. There is no need to deny any negatives, like fear. It will suffice to affirm positive thoughts, like faith, until they become inner feelings. For instance, you do not need to say "There is no fear in my life." Instead you may affirm "There is faith in my life; I believe in God."

After I learned the truth about God and my real Self, I quit drinking, then smoking and later became a complete vegetarian while constantly exercising to keep in good shape. I learned to appreciate my body and decided to harm it no more. Instead, I began to respect it, thanking it for housing me. I became aware that my body is the vehicle I am using to have my human experience. Of course, these changes did not happen overnight. It has taken me 17 years to get where I am. But it took me 42 years of my life to get where I had been.

The consequences of my previous way of life were disastrous, not only for me, but also and especially for my loved ones. This resulted from my choosing disconnectedness from God and losing control over my entire life. I became disconnected from God at a conscious level, because of my adopted wrong beliefs.

You need not go through my difficult and stormy experiences in order to learn what I am now sharing with you. On the other hand, it is entirely useless to try to know the future except, of course, to make forecasts based on scientific data that may or may not be accurate. Do not waste your time and money on sources of information that offer you a look at the future through a commercial, nicely elaborated window.

Suppose for a moment that you could get to know your future through any of those commercialized means and were able to identify the good things that would happen to you. Those things would cease immediately to be good, because you would already know them, and so the delightful element of surprise would disappear. We create joy when things actually happen in the present—not when we speculate that they *might* happen.

Now think about the utility of knowing in advance the bad things that will happen to you. If you could prevent them from happening, this version of your future would cease to be your future, because you would have prevented them from happening. Something very different would happen instead. But if you cannot prevent those bad things from happening, you will then follow a very rugged path waiting for them inevitably to happen.

So you see, there is no use in trying to find out about

our future, to get to know the coming *heres* and *nows*, even if it were possible. The whole Universe is perfect; there is complete balance in it and no reason for us to worry about the future. We have been provided a mind in order to think ahead, to visualize the future into being or to imagine future events into existence. This is true planning for the future. We can decide what it is we shall be doing in the coming *here and now* when it becomes the current *here and now*.

Why should we have faith as the antidote for fear? We fear that the things we desire might not happen, might not become true—and that those things we fear will happen. We may think that we have always had bad luck, which becomes reason enough to sustain the fear. We experience insecurity and uncertainty only because we are not supporting the idea that there is a Power greater than we are, which we can use! Ernest Holmes, author of *The Science of Mind*, constantly affirms this in all his writings.

Maybe we do not buy the idea of a Creator of all there is in the Universe, to which we are all connected because It is the Cause and we are the Effect; and maybe we do not believe that this Creator will certainly take care of the children created by and with Its Intelligence. This apparent separation from such a power is the cause of fear. But the separation happens only in our minds—for we are not actually separated.

Once we overcome this imaginary separation and disconnectedness, and once we recognize that we are one with God and that we are within God and that God is in us, we shall understand why there is no reason to have fear. You can live the moment you are "in" with certainty that this Great Provider, who is all Love and is in you, is there to support you, to sustain you. This belief removes fear from our physical life-experience.

There is no need of fear, just as there is no need to develop unnecessary anxiety that is also taking from you the peace you need in order to have happiness in the *here and now*. If the solution is to develop faith and to have it, why is it that it is not easy to experience the sensation that faith is truly with us? Why isn't it easy to feel the certainty that comes when it is there? If so many people think they have faith, why can't they use it? Having faith is not just *saying* that we have it.

Faith is a constant action from within that results from genuine trust in the idea of not being separated from God, of being constantly and consciously aware that God is within us, that God is all Love—Love for us! Nothing is so much to be trusted as faith, because it always works, one way or the other. All we need to do is to learn how to use it.

We are one with God and one with all other living expressions in the Universe. God is within and around us. We are not outside the Universe or separated from it. We are within it. The Universe is not only some idea you get used to in watching the night skies in the backyard of your home. The Universe is the mind and the body of God.

We should be grateful to the many individuals who have given testimony of their near-death experience (NDE). Thanks to them, we now confirm that there is *more* after so-called physical death, which many humans still believe to be a complete blackout, a total termination. After reading several books published on the subject and watching several videotapes with personal presentations of the individuals who have had NDE, I made some assumptions which I would like to share:

1. Feelings and emotions are entirely different things. Feelings appear to belong to the spiritual entity, to the im-

mortal in us, while emotions seem to be only reactions related to the physical experience. The first continue with the spiritual being according to the declarations of the witnesses, who describe the "feelings of love, of peace, of understanding" they experienced. At the same time, the sprirual entity does not experience emotions, due to the fact that after "dying," it is liberated from the physical environment, from the physical body, which was prepared to react to external stimuli—a reaction that would always vary according to the individual interpretation of the experienced stimuli.

Note how many individuals' testimonies specify that, some time after dying, feelings of peace and feelings of love are identified. Feelings are the subtle ways in which the soul operates, in which our immortal Inner Self, now without a body, *feels!* No more fear, no more anger. One gets into a dimension of permanent joy. All distress and stress have disappeared and are not experienced any more! Emotions such as anxiety, guilt, resentment, fear, anger and the like seem to belong to the physical environment and to be, in a broad sense, physical tools to prevent damage (or further damage) to oneself and to others within the physical environment.

2. All "witnesses" remember their human experiences, with a wealth of details. They did not forget the experiences they lived and what they learned! This confirms that the memory is in the soul, in the spiritual being that was having a multitude of human experiences. The memory is not in the brain cells, inheriting information from generation to generation of cells, as is currently believed. The memory belongs to *the real me*, to *the real you*. We keep it with us when we leave our physical bodies. Better said, the spiritual entity was only using a body equipped with

a computer, the brain, something like our individual PC, which could be defined as the "hardware"—because the software goes with us. We carry with us all the files that once seemed to be within the physical body.

3. We think. We are *constantly* thinking. But we are not aware who or what *the thinker* is. Many people believe that the thinker is the brain. Again, the brain is only like a PC. The thinker is *us*—you and me: the *real* you; the *real* me. Not our physical bodies. That thinker keeps on going with the spiritual entity—with the immortal and real you and me. This is another confirmation that we are not the body. The body does not think by itself. It is only a tool used by the spiritual being as a vehicle to manifest and experience the human condition, the physical environment on Earth.

4. Many testimonies indicate that the "witnesses" that had the NDE were able to see and listen without the physical eyes and ears. However, it seems that without the physical body, it is not possible to touch, smell and taste. All these testimonies confirm what we have been longing for: that after the physical "death," we continue to be! Ernest Homes, in *The Science of Mind*, makes the following comment:

> To suppose that the objective faculties die with the brain, is to suppose that the brain thinks and reasons. This is proved to be false through the experience of death itself, for if the *brain* could think, it would think on and on forever. No, it is not the *brain that thinks*. The *thinker* thinks through the brain perhaps, but of itself the physical brain has no power to think or feel. Detach the brain and it will not formulate ideas nor

work our plans. THE *THINKER* ALONE CAN THINK!*

In any case, our awareness of being, our intelligence, our memories, our feelings and our faculties to see and to listen continue with us, in order to experience other dimensions of life. We are immortal! We have access to an inner certainty that our personal life will continue beyond physical death. I like the way Deepak Chopra shares another of his assumptions in his book *Ageless Body, Timeless Mind*: We are not victims of aging, sickness and death. These are part of the scenery, not the seer, who is immune to any form of change. This seer is the spirit, the expression of eternal being.

*Ernest Holmes, *The Science of Mind* (New York: G. P. Putnam's Sons, 1938), pp. 376–77.

8

The Magic Triangle

I F forgiveness equals peace in the now, and faith in the future also equals peace in the now, what do we do in the *here and now*, the present moment, in the present place, besides being in peace? When we reach this level, we are beginning to set the stage for happiness, because one thing is true: we cannot be happy if we are not first peaceful. Let us be eager to understand this, and let us give it a name. Let me suggest that we call it *The Magic Triangle*—but *magic* in the purest sense of the word. It might be represented as follows:

Forgiveness for the past;

Peace in the *here and now*; and

Faith in the Future.

After achieving peace in the *here and now*, anybody becomes able to experience happiness, enthusiasm, joy and —finally—the maximum encounter with the divine inner characteristic: *love*! At the end of this chapter you will find a chart that better illustrates the whole idea.

You might be asking yourself how you can achieve all this. Almost everybody writing about metaphysics, New Thought or self-help will recommend that you meditate for 20 minutes at least twice a day. Words can hardly describe the benefits of meditation. Perhaps they will not be obvious immediately, but they will become so with some perseverance. In fact you may, with time, come to depend on your meditation sessions as much as you depend on air, food or sleep.

This is certainly the case with me. It is after my daily meditation that I usually perceive a clear picture of what I want to do during the day, and I always end up doing the right thing. It is also after I have meditated that my thoughts are creative, conclusive and definitely not the usual chattering within the brain. When you meditate, consciously aware of the *here and now*, you are halting that chattering, because you get yourself in a state of stillness.

You think better in the morning, after a good night's sleep. In the same way, after halting the chattering—after some good time of stillness—your mind, your Real Self, may better express itself through your physical brain and manifest excellent thinking and right choices and, consequently, the right *outcome* for your life.

I suggest that you make a serious effort to discover your own way to meditation, because each of us differently interprets and practices it. I found very good ideas in the book *Journey of Awakening: A Meditator's Guidebook*, by Ram Dass. Meditation is the way you can achieve what we have been considering, because you will receive from your Voice Within the guidance you may need.

By now you know the importance of forgiveness as well as the importance of faith to secure your peace in the *here and now*. But what kind of *peace* are we talking about? We are speaking of *spiritual* peace—the kind that leads you on to intellectual, physical, emotional and environmental peace. Without first establishing spiritual peace—

which could first of all be defined as your plain recognition of what you are, a *spiritual being*—you will hardly enjoy peace in a holistic sense on a permanent basis. It is this peace, developed as an inner feeling, that builds the foundation for your happiness. It is *magic* because once you secure it, you can decide at any time to be happy and *you will be happy*—at all times if you wish.

This happiness is sustained by your awareness of what you are: a spiritual being doing exactly what you are supposed to do in the *here and now*, based on the vision described in the next chapter. In addition, this triangle (forgiveness, peace, faith) will also seem virtually magic, because at this point you will develop a dramatic enthusiasm that will create your well-deserved joy for your human experience, allowing you to feel pure love for yourself, for others and for Nature as a whole.

Now you can *share* love because you already *have* it. You gave it to yourself first. It has been demonstrated. You cannot share what you do not have; but you have it now! And now that you can share the love you have, give it away in the many ways love can be given. Hugging and kissing your spouse, your children, your relatives, your friends is just an example. Support them, assist them. Do not forget that all the love—and in general all the good—that *can* be given, if *not* given, *gets wasted!* A friend of mine shared with me the expression "My love for you is second-hand, because I gave it to me first!" He told me that he read it in a book by Peter McWilliams.

I think that every good that comes out of us is second-hand. If we do not have it, how can we share it?

Now you have identified which of your beliefs are not serving you well and you are getting ready to drop them off from your system of beliefs, making a paradigm shift. You are getting ready to adopt those beliefs that strengthen your certainty that there is no evil in the Universe, and you are enhancing the efficiency of your process for growing wiser.

Now you will prove that your thoughts define your attitude, that your attitude defines your behavior and that your behavior in turn reflects your thoughts. So the vision of your future previously discussed, and explained in the next chapter, not only will give direction to your life but also will give meaning to your current *here and now*. If you have meaning for the present moment, you do not hesitate to act. You know it. Then, you just go for it!

If you are at peace, if you are happy, nothing can keep you from demonstrating to yourself your intellectual and physical skills, doing what you have to do now, maintaining the direction of your life, accomplishing your short-, medium- and long-term goals. You will no longer suffer for what you do not have, but will rather enjoy what you do have—and you will know that you can have exactly the kind of prosperity you desire.

In his book *The Art of Worldly Wisdom*, Baltasar Gracián shares the aphorism ''Use human means as though divine ones didn't exist, and divine means as though there were no human ones.'' Gracián makes clear that unless we have the willingness to do whatever is necessary to accomplish what we want for our lives, using all the resources available, we are forced to conclude that we really do not want what we say we want—in which case we might have developed the wrong vision. Let's not allow this to be the case. Let's develop a good vision for the remainder of our human experience.

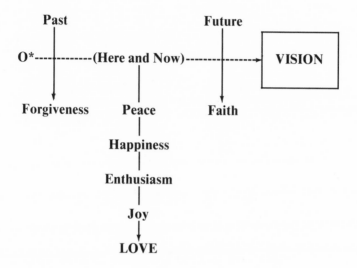

Past   **Future**

O*-------------(Here and Now)------------→ | **VISION** |

Forgiveness   **Peace**   **Faith**

Happiness

Enthusiasm

Joy

LOVE

*This represents the birth date or the date of conception.

9

A Vision for the Future

How do we secure happiness, enthusiasm and joy for life in our future—the coming heres and nows? I would say:

1. By living with a purpose—the purpose that will give direction to our life and, as a consequence, meaning as well to the *here and now*; and

2. By ending the false attitude of being against ourselves (at least unconsciously) by not doing the right thing—that is, changing our lives by changing our thinking; learning "how to think" and then making our innermost desires become true.

What is missing then? If we have been able to solve the past and do not fear the future, then what is left? *Direction*. Most people do not have direction. Many do not know yet where they want to go. Sometimes we do not even know what we *want*. The most common reason why people fail to achieve their goals is: their lack of any! So, let us add a vision to our list in order to get direction. Let us develop a clear vision of the rest of our lives.

Have you noticed that we do not take a trip in a vehicle without defining first where we want to go, and then someone is always in charge of staying on course?

We generally know where we are going with vehicles such as ships, planes, trains and cars; be we seldom define in advance a destination for *ourselves*, the unity of our spiritual being with the vehicle which is our human body. We do not define our destination because we always wind up going somewhere anyhow. However, if we decide on a destination, we not only enable ourselves to go where we want to go, but we may enjoy better control over our lives. We will enjoy having direction and being in charge of keeping control of the journey, like keeping control of the steering-wheel in a car.

When we do not decide on a destination, there is no course to worry about. This seems easier than deciding what we want for our lives. It is then up to you to opt for a definite destination and control the course of your life or simply to allow yourself to go with the flow. The option is yours. In both cases you can be happy; but keep in mind that the latter—not deciding a destination—leads you to places or situations you might not enjoy, because they are not what you wanted, what you *could* have decided but *did* not. (You may, of course, end up enjoying the unexpected destination. Again, the option is yours.)

So you will still be using your unlimited freedom in not determining a vision of the life you would like to live.

One can build the vision for the future by first laying the foundation *or* one can first identify the vision and later on put the foundation in place. But *it is very important* to have a vision of what we truly want for the rest of our lives. Developing such a vision can be done by writing down a clear "picture" of it. Remember that in this way we are giving both direction to the remainder of our physical experience and meaning to each *here and now* we live.

Knowing where we are going allows us to decide exactly

what to do in this *here and now*. It means that we have already identified our purpose in life. It means that we do not need to wander around any more, looking for something to do without getting somewhere in the end. Because, not knowing where we want to go and what we want to do with the rest of our lives is like calling the travel agency and asking for a plane ticket without specifying a destination. The voice at the other end of the line will ask, "Where do you want to go?" If we do not know, how can we possibly want to travel or ask for a plane ticket?

Don't be surprised, but most of us do not know where we want to go during the rest of our lives; however, we know we don't want to die soon, because a voice within is telling us that there is something pending, something to do, a purpose to accomplish, before the unavoidable transition.

We still need to manifest That which is expressing in us! We want to live many years, we want to complete the journey, even if we do not know yet where (and when) we want to go. So, what would you like to do for the rest of your life? If you choose to "go with the flow," you want your life to be just like that. This is totally correct, if you are aware of the rest of the options available to you.

If you feel the opposite—you think there is need of a clearly identified purpose in life and are not sure you can identify the right one now—at least you can start by creating a temporary one. This could very well be a basic identification of the true purpose of your human experience and how to accomplish it. The result will enable you to devote some specific time to identifying the vision that you desire for your future. Do not *generate* one; instead, use meditation and your intuition to *identify* the right vision.

It is important to know and always remember that when the time comes and you feel it necessary, you can change the vision you might have developed for your life and of how to accomplish it. You are free to do so. What I am trying to clarify is that in order to avoid later regrets, there is no risk or any other reason to be afraid of developing a version of a vision now. Wasting part of the totality of our lives without a purpose when we wanted to have one is not for those who have an expanding mind—that is, those of us who recognize that everything in the Universe has a purpose; and there is no doubt that having this human experience is for a great purpose, such as expressing what we really are through making a contribution to the evolutionary process. We need to become a little bit more active actors to avoid being simple passive spectators.

We are the minds that want to be transcendent, excelling in our roles as human beings, making a difference for humanity, because for us, it is the only way to give meaning to life and to encounter and practice givingness. Developing a vision for the rest of your life is like creating a center of gravity that will produce intense energy to pull you, to mobilize you, to keep you focused in your life. You will see how, if genuine, the vision of the rest of your life will demand your total commitment to an expanding path that, like a tremendous source of strength, will be opened only when you have achieved exactly what you wanted.

The vision of our future is our big goal, whatever the goal may be for any one of us. All of our achieved short-, medium- and long-term goals, put together in their sequence and their sum, become what we freely choose to be as humans!

Many writers have already expressed that there is no place to go to be happy—because happiness is (or is not) in us all along the pathway, all along the journey, and not at the end of our human experience!

If this is so, what are we going to do to keep ourselves happy every *here and now*, from this current one until the last one, in which we shall return our body to nature? What if we were able to identify the vision of, and for, the rest of our lives just as we might perceive and effectively elaborate a plan—a plan developed by ourselves, the plan that we know we can always change if we want to? Wouldn't it give us direction? Wouldn't it give meaning to this *here and now*—even a sense of certainty? Of course it would! The utilization of this idea has given direction to my life and plenty of meaning to each moment of it.

Let us now try to collect all the pieces of our lives and put them together, focused in one single vision—an activity similar to putting together a puzzle that comes in a cardboard box with a picture of the completed puzzle on the cover. If the picture of the whole puzzle were not included, you would hardly know what to do with the pieces. It is the same with your life now; it has a lot of pieces, and you do not know what to do with them. By defining a vision for your life, projecting a narrative of your future as you now think it could be, you put together all the pieces of the puzzle and you get the guiding picture for the rest of your life.

This complete picture, better than a lot of words, besides giving you the direction needed, empowers you as if it were your treasure map. It gives meaning to your *here and now*, because you will live each *here and now* with the end in mind, and the picture becomes your "life control manual," because with it you will be in total control. And you will hardly lose that control again, however much you might have lost in the past.

For many people the *here and now* is just the right moment to *suffer*, to be *unhappy*. You can change this; it all depends on you. Just remember that you can always choose the opposite of anything, because you are free to do whatever you want with all you have, with all you possess—that is, with your *here and now*. This is all you really have.

I would like now to call your attention to an important factor: *the consequences*. Everything we choose to do has consequences, good or bad. It is most important to keep in mind, and the beautiful side of it is that if *this moment* is all we have, we can improve everything with the new vision of our future. Once we have direction for our life, everything and every *here and now* will have meaning. Can you imagine this in its real magnitude?

We will know exactly what to do. We will not be wandering, trying to figure out what to do or where to go. We shall know! We shall be certain. We shall be happy doing what we know we are *meant* to do, right where and when we are. We shall be happy doing what we always *wanted* to do, as spiritual beings that are having human experiences, despite our physical age and circumstances.

We can always change our minds. Yes! Isn't it wonderful? As you've already seen, since the vision is yours, because you freely identified and developed it, you can do with it anything that you please—modify or change it, any time. Whatever makes you feel more comfortable, whatever your inner voice tells you to change, *do it*—because you always have the choice.

You are not tied to anybody or anything in this human experience that you do not want to be tied to; you are not tied to any vision that might not completely satisfy you. Besides, nobody can live your life for you. You may only want to introduce adjustments to the vision, especially when you find out that what you have been doing is not exactly what you really want and that variation is possible, and differences can be adjusted.

Developing a vision is not an easy task and is not an easy process. You understand that if you are now living without a vision you will go anywhere life takes you—but you might end up experiencing situations you never desired, even if you are very creative in reacting to them as you experience them. Developing a vision for the rest of your life, on the other hand, is a matter of getting in touch with the real You, with your inner Self, with that "little voice within," and listening carefully. It will clearly give you the right clues to identify your purpose in life and the details on how to integrate your vision. Then it will just be a matter of going after it.

There is a simple process that could help you get started. You can try it without risk of losing anything—not even the time and effort expended, because in the process you will learn very interesting things about yourself. This will help you identify some important portion of yourself for your future through your current wants, which result from your current thoughts and beliefs. To establish the direction you feel is best, from your inner point of view, you need first to identify your wants in the most accurate possible way, then identify the right thing to do or the right place to go to get them. You can also keep on adjusting your wants according to the changes that come to mind, always inspired by "the voice within."

One of the ways your inner voice speaks to you is through that strong feeling of "this is it!" You do not need logical reasons to know if the idea you are considering is what you want. The same is true when you reject other ideas that may be supported by logical reasons, when you feel that you simply do not want them. Of course, the best situation is to feel that inner inclination to an idea that you also considered logically supported. In any case, I prefer to trust my inner voice rather than all the reasons in the world—because I know what it is that is within me, and I rely on it.

To begin the process, I would suggest that you make the decision of accepting *the concept of change*, because change is a key element of your freedom of choice. If we did not have the right and ability to change, we would be forced to be consistent with our previous decisions as we learned in the past to be. We could find ourselves very unhappy throughout our lives for having failed to change.

In the following paragraphs I will suggest a procedure that might help you to identify your vision for the rest of your life. Remembering that you can change your mind at any time, feel free to repeat the same procedure time and again until you are satisfied with what you have been able to identify as the completely desirable vision for the rest of your life, producing, later on, a written version of it (see p. 88).

Think for a moment about an individual who decided to commit suicide. Does he have to be consistent with his decision, or can he change his mind? I think you will agree with me that he can change his mind at any time. And so can you! It is probable that some choices you have made will lead you to a virtual suicide, such as abusing alcohol, smoking, overeating, gambling, overworking, drug abuse, worrying, anger—but you can change at any time, right?

You can recover the balance of your life—the control of it—at any time, if you change your mind. You need not be unhappy: just change your mind. It does not matter what choice of lifestyle you have been supporting: you can change your mind and your choice at any time.

Here is the process that might identify your current wants: Get a sheet of paper on which you will list all the important things you want now for your future, or use the pages of this book that are designated for this purpose (see pages 84–86).

You can title this first page **"What I really want is:"** and number each item (such as #1 for "Want to finish the Spanish Language courses," #2 for "Want to learn how to fly a small plane," #3 for "Want to teach in universities," and so on) until all your goals, wishes or desires are included in the list.

You may end up collecting 20 items—the total amount really does not matter. But do not forget to number each one of them. This might take you a week or more to complete, but that is all right; go slowly. You have probably spent quite some years living without direction. You can afford a few more days without major inconvenience for not having a vision. So take it easy.

Try to list everything you have always wanted because you need it or because you just wish it. Everything you always wanted means *everything*: from getting married, having children, buying a house, getting another job, to moving to another country. And do not share your list with anybody. This is *your* list. It is just for you. It is You with You. If you share it with anyone, you are going to "contaminate" it!

The next step is to create a second list that you may title: **"Why?"** Your first list was *"What I really want is:"* and your second is *"Why?"* Using the same numbers you used in the first list for each given item, write down your completely honest reason for wanting each of them. At the right side of the number write what would be for yourself the most satisfactory reason. For example, #1: "Because that will help me conform to the requirement of my job, promotion/assignment in Latin America." #2: "I do not really have a reason to want to fly a small plane now. I just thought of it. I do not see what the benefit might be, mainly because I am a little afraid of heights.''

In this latter case, you will *not* carry #2 over to the third list, which we are about to consider. What is important is that the reason you have for wanting something or not wanting it is accepted by you, is good enough for you. If you doubt whether your reason is a good one, leave the item on the list. Some time later you will find out if you really want it or not.

You will now notice something interesting: if your first list had 20 items, after you complete your second list the number of items may be dramatically reduced to a few because you are not giving yourself adequate or acceptable reasons for wanting most of the items in the first list. You really do not want them! Now you are closing the gap by getting to know what you *really* want, and this will lead to identifying what to do for the rest of your life, because you are presumably identifying the major things you want to do, finish or accomplish in the short, medium and long term.

Now let's create the third list. This list is going to be titled: **"What am I doing to get it/What can I do to get it?"** Here you will write down, beside the corresponding number, what you are actually and currently doing to get your wants *or* what you consider you could do to get them.

First, you will notice that you are probably doing *nothing* to get the want you are dealing with at that moment, and this will cause you to identify actions that you must perform if you really desire it. So identify an action and write it down.

Second, even though you may have been doing a few things to get the want you are dealing with now, you may have the feeling that you really do not desire it, that you do not wish to involve yourself in additional effort for it. In this case, you really do not desire it, and you will not include it in the document containing the written version of your vision. There can also be an item for which your current action is satisfactory to you. Thus you do not need to identify additional action unless you feel you must.

You will finish the whole process with two or three items left from the original 20, and these are *what you really want*. These few items that are left suddenly transform you. They become very important to you. They begin to prioritize your life. They are the basis, the foundation, and your guide for starting to build a vision for the rest of your life.

What you have identified are the things that you really want the most, the things you always wanted to do or to have, the things you really wish to work for. By identifying these things, you are identifying the most important portion of the rest of your life. You may start whenever you feel comfortable enough to be responsible to yourself:

What I Really Want Is:

_____

_____

_____

_____

_____

_____

_____

_____

_____

_____

_____

_____

_____

_____

_____

_____

Why?

_____

_____

_____

_____

_____

_____

_____

_____

_____

_____

_____

_____

_____

_____

What Am I Doing to Get It/What Can I Do to Get It?

_____

_____

_____

_____

_____

_____

_____

_____

_____

_____

_____

_____

_____

_____

_____

_____

This is what responsibility means to me. The same meaning can be useful for you, because you have to answer to yourself for your own actions at all times, whether you realize it or not—because the choices you make take you to where you are in life. From now on what will count is the kind of choices you will make with your new tool of identified goals. The worthwhile selection of these choices is your mission toward reaching your vision.

You may repeat this same procedure every six months, or as you feel the need to do so. You will find out that the main items do not change dramatically. In fact, the changes may be very small or insignificant. A new item or two may be added; or an important one that in the past seemed relevant may completely disappear. In any case, this is the way we start getting closer to a final version of the vision for our future!

Suddenly, one day, you will know with certainty what it is you want to do with the rest of your lfie. You will have identified what for you will be the highest purpose for the rest of your human experience. Then repeating the process from time to time will keep you in control of your vision and focused on your destination and on the direction and the meaning of your life; and, of course, it will strengthen your determination.

Let's suppose, theoretically, that you have identified that you always wanted to teach some discipline. This will guide you to integrate a vision for the rest of your life, give direction to your life and give meaning to this moment, this *here and now*, because now you know what you can do in it. By the time you get your teaching degree (if you do not have it yet) and you are ready to start teaching, you can use this same process of revising and confirming your vision again.

Sometimes you may have to deviate from your course temporarily because a relative dies, something urgent arises, or a major change poses itself; but the diversion will be temporary. You may have to work more, but you will not be lacking direction at any moment. Also, tough decisions may be called for, such as choosing between a good job offer and the completion of your studies. However, having your vision clearly identified will make your decision a snap. What most counts is that you live a life of satisfaction by using your freeodm of choice to change or not to change, consciously aware that in the only moment you are alive, you are doing exactly what you *want*, because it is what you have freely chosen to do!

After your moments of meditation, when you enable yourself to listen to your voice within, to your real Self, what you are really using is your intuition, the internal tuition, the internal feedback that originates in the God within. All this plays an enormous role in the identification and definition of a vision, but more importantly in the identification of *what to do* to achieve your vision. This is your mission toward reaching your vision. So do not forget to meditate daily, or at least at the pace that you feel best suits your needs.

At this point, putting a well-defined "picture" of your conclusions in writing makes it worth experiencing. You get the meaning of life you have been searching for. You will waste no more *heres* and *nows*. Putting your vision in writing will make of that vision a center of gravity that attracts sufficient universal energy to support you in making that vision happen. Your mission toward reaching your vision is a possible mission because you will be doing what you believe is the right thing for you to do.

If you share your vision with your family, your friends

or associates, do it when it is complete—not before. Even in these conditions you might receive expressions of surprise or remarks of reluctance to accept your decisions; but unless the comments are acceptable, do not change the version of your vision because of their comments. You might end up "contaminating" it. However, it is good to share one's vision. The advantage of sharing the contents of your vision, totally or partially, is that you might get the support and cooperation of those authentically connected to you.

If one day within the next five or ten years you discover, with different information received from either your inner Self or external sources, that you want to do something entirely different, do not feel tied down to your current choice. You are allowed to change then in the same way that you can change now. You can *always* change, anything, at any time. God created us totally free to choose, to the point that we can even choose whether to respond or not to God. You can easily prove this assertion by looking around at the many people who have chosen *not* to respond to God or to themselves. We are not intended to be marionettes. God is within us; we are not separate entities from God. We are only individuals within the same Great Entity—within God as one with God—but individually, and entirely, free to choose how to manifest and experience this physical world.

Choose to fulfill your life—to take what you want from it and the most out of it!

10

The Thought School

I can choose to control what I think. With controlled thinking, I can adopt new beliefs and discard old ones. I can interpret freely and differently at any time, on every occasion—even repeated occasions. I can also get myself to discover *what I know*. Similarly, I can choose to exert no control over my thoughts, to react based on my previously learned beliefs and to live without discovering what *I know*.

Let me explain this.

What I know is beyond anything I currently believe or think, either spontaneously *or not*. If I do not learn *how* to think, I might never, during my physical experience, be able to discover what *I know*. As I am spirit in essence, you will agree with me that there is no limitation in my inner knowledge.

However, all of that knowledge is in my higher Self, in the *real* me. It has not been transferred as ''software'' to my brain, which is a temporary tool within the human vehicle, my body. I need to take the decision of making the effort to control my thoughts, to become able to access that inner knowledge completely, because up to now the access has been limited to really small fractions of its vastness.

We have not yet learned how to properly use our thinking and how to manage it, how to get the best out of it, to the point that scientific statistics affirm that we only use an average of 5 to 15 percent of our brain capacity. We have not yet learned how to use this inherent faculty —even though it is subject to our will because it is within us, with the easiest possible access. Having learned to manage big external powers, such as electricity, nuclear reactions, and the elements of combustion, we need to seriously face the importance of learning how to manage the greatest power of all: *Thought*.

We have business schools, where we learn how to manage business, but we do not have "thought schools," where we could go to learn how to manage thought before we learn how to manage other important skills in life. However, there is no skill that is as important as learning how to manage thought, which is the root cause of everything. Why couldn't we have a thought school, specializing in the art of thinking?

Thought is a power, because it was thought that created the universe and everything in it, manifesting unlimited intelligence. Everything we see, touch, smell, hear or taste was created by thought, including all that we do *not* see, touch, smell, hear or taste. As though this were not enough, you have only to look around you to see that everything created by human hands, with or without tools, is also the result of thought and the output of intelligence, imagination and evolution.

The thought of God created us in Its image and likeness, and because of this, we have the same creative power. However, we use this power in a very random manner—not in the systematically organized way in which it could be used, the equivalent of knowing *how* to think. Instead, we substitute the continuing tradition of having our human life experienced only with the limited "what to think" learned.

There is no denying that the human race needs more thinkers, more individuals specialized in the practice of conscious thinking and in the exercise of creative and guided thought. This is especially important for those leading humanity to higher levels of development, growth and evolution. Everybody needs to become an expert in proper thinking—to understand the Truth and claim the joy possible during this physical experience. Learning how to think, how to manage thought, is to contribute to the evolutionary process.

I think that we are at the threshold of a giant leap, the beginning of a transition that one can see is now happening in the world. We are beginning to find out that we already are what we want to become, that we already are where we want to go, that we do not need to get *closer* to God, but to become consciously aware of the closeness in which we *already are*, because of *what* we are.

All that we need do to complete the leap is to learn *how* to think. We do not need to think *about divine things*, but to think *from our Divine Selves!* As Ernest Holmes says in *The Science of Mind*:

> Know your own mind. Train yourself to think what you wish to think; be what you wish to be; feel what you wish to feel, and place no limit on Principle!
>
> *The words which you speak would be just as powerful as the words which Jesus spoke, if you knew your word was the Law whereunto it was sent, but you must KNOW this WITHIN and not merely accept it with your intellect.* If you have reached a point where the inner consciousness believes, then your word is simply an announcement of Reality!*

---

*Ernest Holmes, *The Science of Mind* (New York: G. P. Putnam's Sons, 1938), p. 188.

At this point, I should like to acknowledge my indebtedness to this book and its author. I can highly recommend Dr. Holmes' teachings; for me, they have offered the very best understanding and enjoyment of the human experience.

11

The Universal Process

T HE physical universe—what we see—and the invisible, which we do not see, are the thought or "word" of God made manifest. The way in which the thought or word is made manifest is through the perfect process of the Law—another way of saying that Universal Intelligence, God, Spirit or Consciousness, *knowing* Itself, created a medium to manifest Itself to Itself! This medium is the Law, Its Law, the Universal Law—"the Law of Mind in action," as Ernest Holmes was fond of calling it. Those of us who understand the industrial or manufacturing sequence of

Input----------PROCESS----------Output

as well as those who work with computers, who have learned that the *inputs* introduced to a computerized process, after being "processed," become the *outputs*, will easily understand that the thought of God or the word of God—the cause—is processed within a *medium* that produces an effect—the outputs.

When the universe was created by pure Intelligence, by

pure thought, it was created through a medium, a Universal Law, that in orderly fashion produced all that the thought or word of Intelligence was decreeing. Everything in the universe was produced to follow an organized process of evolution. Hence, it is said that evolution is the *outcome* of intelligence and not its cause, as many scientists still tend to believe.

Earlier we noted that we have the same characteristics in ourselves that Universal Intelligence possesses, because we are made of Its same essence; we are made in Its image and likeness. Consequently, we also have access with our thought to the same Universal Law, the one that processes thought—the input—as cause, and produces (or manifests) the output as the effect—any effect we choose.

In other words, the thought of God produced the universe and everything in it through the Law. We, as spiritual beings, as extensions of God having human experiences, produce those experiences with our thoughts, because everything we think, consciously or unconsciously, may become a "cause" that through the Law will produce an effect, an output, an outcome, a result. This is a triune picture of the Universal manifestation and of the individual manifestation.

Here we see the main reason why it is so important that we learn how to think; for by not doing so, we have produced through ignorance a world of disease, scarcity, violence and many other destructive effects with the "what to think" that we learned, the same "what to think" that is still transmitted to new generations in many places of this world. We ought constantly to remember that there is only One God and that evil as such does not exist: the "evil" we experience is only the negative manifestation or outcome of our ignorance. Consequently there is only One Power in the Universe—not two—as we have erroneously learned from the wrong beliefs we have adopted.

It is my understanding that what exists is our total freedom on the one hand and, on the other, the fact that we have erroneously learned to have negative thoughts and to hold with obstinacy to wrong beliefs. These negative thoughts are processed and manifested by the universal medium, and we interpret them as the manifestation of evil; but they are only the manifestation of what we think or of what we believe.

To summarize: there is only One Power and, because of our unlimited freedom, two ways of using it. Since our thoughts are manifested through the medium of the Universal Law, if we think in positive terms—that is, if we truly know "how"—we shall produce in our lives all the positive conditions or effects we desire. However, if we think or believe in the negative ways learned in the past— that is, the "what to think" we inherited—the outcome will be what we do not desire, as negative as our thoughts or our beliefs, because the medium of the Universal Law, by reason of its very nature, is totally obedient and as readily manifests positive thoughts as negative ones, without qualification. During our human experience we only get what we think, in the way we think it, consciously or unconsciously.

We need a change—a radical change—not to be attained by fighting our predicament but by favoring its opposite, by picturing in our minds new conceptions of the world, of love, of health, of abundance and of peace— conceptions that conform to the perfection of the Universe. We definitely need to learn "how" to think in order to instill the right thoughts, the right inputs, into the Law of God, which is the process that makes them manifest.

We cannot afford to continue thinking garbage, be-

cause the Law, obedient as it is, will produce what we willingly (or unwillingly) communicate to it.

It is true that not every thought of ours is manifested—
which, if it were, would be a disaster, given the quality of
much human thinking! I believe that only those thoughts
to which we add "feeling," filled with interest and real
involvement, are the ones that manifest. But many negative thoughts become manifested simply because we humans have not yet learned how to think, how to manage
thought—because we put a lot of energy in our fears and
other negative thoughts or beliefs.

We need to yield outputs, produced by the Universal
Process, representing only what we really want, what we
really expect, if we have previously changed our thinking.
When we get wrong experiences—or experiences we do
not like—out of this life, we are showing a lack of ability to respond to ourselves, a lack of responsibility; because we now know that we can change for the better;
that is, we can put the right thoughts into the Universal
Medium to get the outputs we desire.

If we change our thinking, we will do the equivalent of
changing seeds: the soil will be the same obedient medium
that will process the new seeds in the same way it processed the previous ones, but the new output will cor-
respond to that of the new seeds, to that of the new
thinking. If we learn how to manage our thought power,
we are automatically deciding a better life for ourselves
and automatically providing better information for future
generations that, with their own creative thought, will improve what they inherit.

We are not blocked by anything from having a Quality Life. Yes, a Quality Life! As a trained Quality expert
of work processes, products and services, I know that we
can improve anything we decide we want to improve.

Quality can also be defined as *"continuous improvement."* This brings us to conclude that "thinking improvement" equals Quality.

We are expansive minds with enormous potential—potential that only now we are beginning to discover and utilize. As a consequence, I dare to affirm that we can have a Quality Life, and that nothing *but ourselves with our current beliefs* is limiting us from having and enjoying it. The reaction to this affirmation should be a radical and complete paradigm shift—a decision to reorient our thoughts to the highest possibilities. Because if we choose goals within a vision beyond ourselves and we accomplish those goals and reach such a vision, we will grow more than we ever expected. We will prove how expansive we are; we will prove the universal harmony prevailing in our lives, we will be using our potentialities. Again, Ernest Holmes in *The Science of Mind* (the capitals are his):

MAN MUST BECOME MORE IF HE WISHES TO DRAW A GREATER GOOD INTO HIS LIFE. . . . EVERY MAN MUST PAY THE PRICE FOR THAT WHICH HE RECEIVES AND THAT PRICE IS PAID IN MENTAL AND SPIRITUAL COIN.*

We need to live focused on our purpose, to stay on the right track and, most importantly, to be "finishers"—those who always finish any initiated thing, those who work hard to complete any project, to accomplish any task. It has been said that what counts is the intention—that once we have the intention, nothing can really keep

*Ernest Holmes, *The Science of Mind* (New York: G. P. Putnam's Sons, 1938), pp. 267, 268.

us from accomplishing what we want. I do not totally agree with that, because it all depends on the *kind* of intention. For instance, if I had the intention to do something wrong, I could—and I should—change that intention at any time, right?

Our knowing how to think enables us to change wrong intentions but also allows us to stay focused on the good ones. Often excellent projects are left unfinished because we do not devote the necessary time to them. Although we may be very intelligent in every other respect, still we do not know how to think, nor do we recognize that humble perseverance is much more effective than intelligence without action.

The point is that we are free to change anything, any time. It does not matter how many changes are made: we have to finish things, finish projects, get results, the desired outputs. Otherwise, how do we know if the idea or ideas were good? We must be guided by the "new thought" not merely to abstain from wrong thinking with guidance, but to become proactive about a new way of living, in which we are constantly growing, constantly happy, constantly expanding.

We need to be conscious that we are already prepared to have whatever we might need to experience a life of satisfaction, a Quality Life. We must have a great human experience, because if we are God's manifestation, we already have a great responsibility—the reponsibility to express God on Earth.

We will not search for things that might hurt or adversely affect others any longer, because we are ready to take responsibilty for our own happiness, which is the most desirable choice we can make! We need to realize that we can truly demonstrate throughout our human experience what we truly are: *Expressions of God on Earth!*

I agree with those who affirm that metaphysics is the psychology of the future, because it is sustained by spiritual truth. The evolution of human thought will confirm this assertion, will prove that we humans are going in the right direction when we choose more and more to depend on Universal Principle, on Universal Truth, instead of on conventional legends and traditional myths, which are no longer sustainable.

Epilogue

I DO not want you to do the wrong thing right the first time, but I wish you to do the right thing right the first time—and every time. This means that by using the information in this book, you will find in yourself the imprint of success written in bold letters, especially if you raise your consciousness to the highest possible level—that is, if you get yourself to discover your higher Self, to experience God!

May you find yourself!

Héctor

About the Author

Héctor Amézquita was born in Guatemala in 1937. A self-taught individual, Héctor joined the largest local retail business firm, D. Weissman Sucs., Ltd., in Guatemala City in 1953 at the age of 15. At 23 he became a partner, and the firm name changed to Weissman & Amézquita Cia. Ltda. Nine years later, Héctor became sole proprietor. He expanded the business, opening a second store and a travel agency.

For three terms he was a Director of the Central Bank of Guatemala (1969–88). In 1981 he became Financial Director of Johnson & Johnson Central America, S.A. In 1982 he liquidated his business in which he had invested 29 years of his life. After several promotions within Johnson & Johnson, Héctor was transferred to the United States as a Total Quality Management Consultant. Operating from Brazil and later Puerto Rico, he then became Director of Total Quality Management for Latin America and the Caribbean.

Héctor retired in 1993, moving to Central Florida, where he studies the Science of Mind. He has two children and two grandchildren. His favorite sport is water-skiing. He is an avid searcher of the Universe and speaks four languages: English, Spanish, Portuguese and French.